THE ENGLISH GRAND TOUR

Artists and Admirers of England's Historic Sites

The English Grand Tour

Artists and Admirers of England's Historic Sites

JULIUS BRYANT

ENGLISH HERITAGE

Frontispiece: James Mason after Augustin Heckell, *The Countess of Suffolk's House near Twickenham* (Marble Hill), 1749

Published by English Heritage, Isambard House, Kemble Drive, Swindon SN2 2GZ
www.english-heritage.org.uk

English Heritage is the Government's statutory adviser on all aspects of the historic environment.

First published 2005

ISBN 1 85074 889 6
Product code 50948

British Library Cataloguing in Publication data
A CIP catalogue for this book is available from the British Library.

Edited and brought to publication by Susan Kelleher and René Rodgers, English Heritage Publishing
Designed by George Hammond
Printed in Belgium by Snoeck-Ducaju & Zoon

For further information about English Heritage and our sites, please contact:
English Heritage Customer Services
PO Box 569
Swindon SN2 2YP
Telephone: 0870 333 1181
Website: www.english-heritage.org.uk

Contents

Preface

Setting forth on the adventure of assembling this visual compendium, the writer had no higher ambition than simply to provide an attractive armchair tour, in alphabetical order, of some of the 412 historic sites now in the care of English Heritage. The richer potential of this subject soon emerged. By including both historic paintings and new photographs of the actual sites *The English Grand Tour* invites potential travellers to see each historic place through artists' eyes, to explore their use of artistic licence and to recognise how artists have influenced our ways of seeing. By including posters, modern paintings, prints and drawings the book also shows how some sites are still a source of inspiration today. Bringing together the artistic and antiquarian responses to historic landmarks should help today's visitors and admirers to enjoy both the sites and the paintings from fresh perspectives. Both intellectually and physically, these special places need to be seen from positions other than those determined by the car park and ticket office.

The choice of title for the book was a deliberate challenge to the normal understanding of the term 'Grand Tour', which usually denotes European travel by wealthy aristocratic men in the 18th century, the social elite on whom the discussion of travel has traditionally focussed. Therefore this book highlights images made widespread through reproduction for a middle-class market intent on travel.

Beyond describing the sites, the introductory text also invites the reader to reflect on the contribution these places made to the rise of popular tourism, with the establishment of regular leisure time and the spread of public transport in the 19th and 20th centuries. The forebears of today's sightseers came for a variety of reasons and brought a wealth of associations to sites that many visitors lack today; their interest had its roots in 18th-century aesthetic theories, in historical fiction and Romanticism. The text encourages consideration of the much wider subject of how English notions of a national landscape and values of 'Englishness' were shaped by historical tourism, among both native travellers and foreign visitors.

The book also recognises the contribution English Heritage is making, through its management of these sites, to our sense of common ownership, our shared values and cultural self-image, at the start of the 21st century. The selection of historic houses, castles and abbeys is confined to those now in the care of English Heritage and so does not include some classic choices of artists, such as Tintern Abbey (in Monmouthshire) or, indeed, the historic building most painted by British artists, Windsor Castle. Given the growth of the book's parameters it does not seek to do more than introduce readers to these sites, artists and issues and the reader is referred to the bibliography for more comprehensive studies.

Acknowledgements

To Susannah Lawson at English Heritage, I am indebted for the invitation to compile this book as a 'sequel' to my study of one artist's views of such sites, *Turner: Painting the Nation* (1996). Her suggestion chimed with my own hopes of mounting an exhibition to mark the 21st birthday of English Heritage that would be a sequel to the exhibition and catalogue *Finest Prospects* (Bryant 1986), a study of fashionable villas from the perspective of sightseeing in outer London in the 18th century. René Rodgers took on editorial responsibility with Susan Kelleher and they have seen the book through to publication with great patience, perseverance, precision and tact, in collaboration with the designer George Hammond. Diana Phillips has been tenacious in her picture research and Lisa Shakespeare coordinated a wealth of potential candidates for illustration while finding more. In their work on English Heritage's collections and interiors my colleagues Amber Xavier-Rowe, Martin Allfrey and Trevor Reynolds gave me space to think.

For help with specific research enquiries I am indebted to Jonathan Coad, Karen Hearn, Charles Hind, Gareth Hughes, Michael Hunter, Richard Linzey, Susan Morris, Tony Musty, Paul Pattison, Cathy Power, David Sherlock, Margaret Timmers, Caroline Carr-Whitworth and Rowena Willard-Wright. Gainsborough's lost view of Landguard Fort is here published for the first time thanks to its discoverer, Anthony Mould, and to the generosity of its private owner. I am especially grateful to the artist Barry Martin for spending time at Battle Abbey and creating his own response to the battlefield of 1066 especially for this volume. The staff at the National Art Library and at the RIBA/V&A Study Rooms at the Victoria & Albert Museum could not have been more helpful. I am also grateful to those private owners of views of their former ancestral homes who have kindly agreed to their paintings being reproduced here.

To the many curators, inspectors, conservators and custodians who have shown me around monuments, castles, abbeys and houses during my working tours over my 21 years with English Heritage as Director of Collections and Chief Curator, I am most grateful for sharing their expertise and enthusiasm. I hope this book may inspire many more to visit and admire the objects of their devotions. At home, to Barbara and Max, as ever, I am grateful for ignoring me when the editors called and Clio beckoned.

Julius Bryant

The English Grand Tour

— The appreciation of England's historic sites —

The term 'Grand Tour' traditionally denotes a lengthy visit to Rome by a young aristocrat in the 18th century, ostensibly to complete his education through studying art and architecture. More often than not it turned into a quest to complete his maturity into manhood by exploring all the worldly temptations he could satisfy with his allowance. Today, the tradition lives on in the concept of the 'Gap Year', where travel broadens the mind much further afield and without the benefit of a watchful tutor. The notion of an 'English Grand Tour' may, therefore, almost sound like a contradiction in terms. In English history the stay-at-home counterpart to the extravagant young aristocrat was the antiquary, the worthy-if-dull country squire, clergyman, lawyer or literary hack with a bent for history and a tendency to archaeology. While the alumni of the Grand Tour savoured their souvenirs of travel, such as 'old master' paintings of the Italian countryside, the antiquaries studied their folios of topographical engravings and learned journals illustrated with vignettes of ruined abbeys, castles and other relics of ancient times. But travel at home was infinitely more affordable than abroad and the sightseers of today in search of their history have a greater variety of forebears than just the connoisseurs who commissioned paintings and the scholars we know from the books they published.

Much of the popular literature that documents the rise of the 'polite tourist' and the commercialisation of leisure travel dates from the late 18th and early 19th centuries. In the 'Age of Reason' ways of looking at landscapes and ruined monuments were articulated into aesthetic theories. The Picturesque helped the admirer to evaluate a view (a 'fine prospect') by the degree to which it resembled a landscape painting by the 17th-century masters, Claude Lorrain, Nicolas Poussin and Gaspard Dughet. The Sublime had a more associative, literary appeal and was used to label the fearful, threatening, solemn or melancholy prospect on which to muse, reassured of one's safety, such as a ruin in a storm at night. The most influential treatises were Edmund Burke's *Philosophical Enquiry into the Origin of Our Ideas of the Sublime and Beautiful* (1757) and William Gilpin's guides and essay *On Picturesque Travel* (1792). This articulation of aesthetic theories opened up connoisseurship, whether of art, architecture or landscapes, from the educated aristocracy and gentry to a growing middle-class market at a time when national consciousness and pride was rising among the English.

Artists catered for both markets, whether illustrating treatises or travel books, producing topographical prospects of towns, country houses or even factories to order, or celebrating their own genius before the inspiration of nature in masterpieces painted without patrons for the prestige of public exhibition. John Constable's classic view of Hadleigh Castle (1829) with the Essex marshes beyond (illustrated on the front cover and p 61) sums up both approaches. The painting is usually described as an expression of his sense of loss at the death of his wife, as a seminal work of the Romantic Movement. Yet it also grew from the antiquarian tradition of admiring and recording ancient sites and the customary educated admirer's response to ruins of reflecting on the transient nature of all man's worldly achievements.

The expansion of the popular press in the 18th century made travel books and engravings after artists' views of sites and prospects available to a much wider audience. The Society of Dilettanti and others sponsored archaeologists and architects to explore and record lost ruins in Greece and Asia Minor for publication in the most luxurious of books; at the same time pocket-size 'companions' could aid the local amateur historian. For example, in Henrietta Pye's *Short Account of the Principal Seats in and about Twickenham* (1756) the author explains in her introduction the trend for young ladies to view England's latest fashionable villas around London:

I have observed that ladies in general, visit those places, as our young gentlemen do foreign parts, without answering any other end, than barely saying they have been there ... These little excursions being commonly the only travel permitted to our sex, & the only way we have of becoming at all acquainted with the Progress of Arts, I thought it might not be improper, to throw together on paper, such remarks as occurred to me.

The determination of young ladies to view the more sublime spectacle of ruined castles could prompt caricatures of polite guides, such as James Green's satirical *Poetical Sketches of Scarborough* (1813), where windswept maids are shown struggling to preserve their parasols and their modesty (*see* pp 108–9).

The spread of historical novels and epic poems, such as Sir Walter Scott's Elizabethan romance *Kenilworth* (1821) and of Alfred, Lord Tennyson's evocation of the Arthurian legend *Idylls of the King* (1859), armed a self-educated audience. Equipped with sufficient associative, if fictionalised, information, a wider public could respond to even the least Picturesque or Sublime architectural remains and seek out more than the antiquarians may have measured. Associations were not only of romantic scenes from history. Patriotic pride could be stirred by the achievements of English Gothic architecture as it was claimed as a national style in preference to the classical tradition.

Ruins from the Anglo-Saxon era carried political connotations. King Alfred was seen as a father of the English nation with its traditions of monarchy limited by Parliament, common law and trial by jury. The fate of the monasteries and establishment of the Church of England was another lesson from history told by its ruins. Shells of abbeys could prompt thoughts on the decline of the Catholic church and of superstition in England. Castles that failed to recover from the Civil War when they were slighted (made indefensible) could also prompt musings on the advantages of Parliament over absolutism, and the benefits of a constitutional monarchy over Jacobitism. At Duncombe Park, for example, prospects of both Rievaulx Abbey and Helmsley Castle were incorporated into the terrace walks planned by the owner in order to encourage his guests to reflect, from a safe distance, on the benefits and legitimacy of the Protestant Hanoverian Whig ideology of the ruling class.

Travel to historic sites became a key part of the growing middle class's popular culture of nationhood. Such patriotic and civic pride was fuelled when the country went to war, most notably against Revolutionary and Napoleonic France (1793–1815). At this time, when civilian travel abroad all but ceased, the hunger to see and understand the nation's landmarks grew and established the deep roots of today's notion of 'heritage'.

Travelling to admire architecture, ancient or modern, is an instinct as old as our ability to build. The Norman nephews and cousins of William the Conqueror built great castles with imposing keeps, such as at Orford, not only for their defence but also to intimidate the displaced Anglo-Saxon nobility. Today's museum directors in hot pursuit of the latest endangered treasure that must be saved for the nation, and who build great extensions to house them, are the direct heirs of the abbots of Hailes, Lindisfarne and Castle Acre with their holy relics. Some of these relics were purchased for great sums abroad, complete with certificates of authenticity before the competitive abbots built new shrines and chapels for the pilgrims they sought to attract. Medieval bishops spent much of their time on the road with their households, visiting their dioceses. Long before Queen Elizabeth I brought her court to stay at Kenilworth, itinerant kings travelled the country from castle to castle to ensure the loyalty of their subjects and to check border and coastal defences. Some abbeys and castles were built on existing trade routes, to encourage settlement and increase revenue from new market towns. Old Sarum, for example, rose close to the intersection of five Roman roads and it was here, for this reason, that William the Conqueror chose to hold the mass demobilisation of his army.

The choice of sites to see was plentiful thanks to their location on the historic routes taken by monarchs, pilgrims, traders and the military. However, until the 1860s, most people travelled by coach along traditional routes linking major towns and by boat around the coast. The range of historic sites and landscape prospects accessible to leisure travellers increased dramatically with the invention of the locomotive. The advent of the railway made such special places available to a much broader and larger public, particularly from the booming new manufacturing towns of the Midlands and the north. The Lake District

Georgina, Countess of Dudley, and friends in front of the Perseus and Andromeda fountain at Witley Court, c 1875, photograph (Weidenfeld and Nicholson Archives)

became a tourist destination in the 1850s, thanks to the railway. However, trains could also bring more direct destruction. With the opening up of Scotland to tourism, the castle at Berwick-upon-Tweed had to be demolished in the 1840s to make way for the railway tracks. Hailes Abbey and Furness Abbey had stations nearby and, where trains ran, hotels soon followed. William Wordsworth and John Ruskin lamented the spread of tourism at Furness, particularly after a hotel was built next to the ruins. A railway poster for Rievaulx Abbey encouraged potential passengers to come and see the new excavations (*see* p 106). At Tintagel the local entrepreneurs lobbied to get a railway station and failed, but instead got a vast station hotel, appropriately named King Arthur's Castle.

Residents of an antiquarian inclination created museums in the 19th century, as at Bolsover Castle and Carisbrooke Castle. In the early 19th century Boscobel House was restored internally in a 17th-century manner in order to meet the interest of sightseers on the trail of Charles II. Merchandise – such as snuff boxes – was made from the boughs of the original Boscobel oak in which Charles II had hid from Oliver Cromwell's search party.

For country houses the potential of a royal visit could inspire owners to invest in architectural expansion and enrichment in the hope of personal advancement. This happened at Audley End and Kirby Hall, though the supreme guests failed to show (*see* pp 14 and 74). The tradition of entertaining royalty and their entourage continued into the Edwardian age; at Witley Court shooting parties for Edward, Prince of Wales (later King Edward VII) could last a week and fill every room with guests and their servants. With the decline of family fortunes uninvited sightseers might include crowds at auctions of contents held over several days, as at Marble Hill in 1824, Kenwood in 1922 and Witley Court in 1938.

— Artists and the allure of historic sites —

The English love of travel and history is reflected in topographical paintings, which reveal a greater love, that of property, both personal and national. In a country where social status and political influence have traditionally derived from the ownership of land, it is not surprising that artists were needed to record achievements, both by families and by the nation at large. Working in a town, away from the pleasures of a rural villa or country house, far from their favourite castles and other ruins symbolic of ancestry, a wealthy landowner would take pride in hanging on his (or her) wall a painting of the estate or a view of the land of his fathers. This seems to be peculiar to this country, for there are far more paintings of rural architecture, whether country houses, cathedrals, castles, gardens or factories, produced here than in continental Europe.

From the 17th century competent painters of landscape, as with portraiture, had to be imported in order to meet the market demand. The distant view of Richmond Castle by Alexander Keirincx (who came from Antwerp) and the similarly semi-panoramic prospect of Pendennis Castle in Falmouth harbour by Hendrick Danckerts (from The Hague) both typify a 'wide-angle' way of seeing the world that Dutch and Flemish artists brought to this country. Keirincx came to London in 1640–1 to paint views of royal castles and palaces for Charles I. Danckerts settled in London after the Great Fire of 1666 and, in 1688, 27 topographical landscapes by him were recorded in the Royal Collection. The more elevated 'bird's eye' prospect, as adopted by Wenceslaus Hollar (from Bohemia) for Boscobel, and by Leonard Knyff (from Haarlem) and Johannes Kip (from Amsterdam) for their engravings of Wrest Park and Hailes Abbey, became the favoured viewpoint for country house portraiture.

In contrast to such comprehensive records by the Dutch and Flemish precision painters, the architectural topographers Samuel and Nathaniel Buck chose more selective and inviting points of view for their survey of over 500 of Britain's antiquities between 1720 and 1750, represented in this book by their views of Kirkham Priory and Berwick. *Buck's Antiquities* (1774) first appeared in five volumes and would have appealed to the same market as *Britannia Illustrata* (1707) by Knyff and Kip. In the text accompanying 84 engravings in his *Antiquities of Great Britain* (1778–81), the painter Thomas Hearne brought an artist's eye to the analysis of medieval architectural styles at a time when the dating of buildings was left to antiquarians and their documents. In this way artists opened up the connoisseurship of buildings to a wider public.

The price of publications by the Buck brothers and by Hearne kept them within the collector's market but their views were soon plagiarised for magazines and volumes published for tradesmen and others aspiring to join polite society. For example, Alexander Hogg's *The Complete English Traveller* (1771) and G A Walpoole's *New British Traveller* (1784) realised the commercial potential of the growing market for topographical tour literature. Fresh commissions for artists came with the ambitious series, the *Beauties of England and Wales*, edited by John Britton and Edward Brayley, published in 27 volumes over 15 years (1801–16), for which artists such as Hearne, John Varley, J M W Turner and Benjamin West supplied a total of 700 views.

Popular engravings encouraged travellers to view not only historic sites but also fashionable gardens. The detailed maps encircled by postcard-sized vignettes of pavilions, bridges and other features produced by the French designer John Rocque for Wrest Park in 1735 and Chiswick House in 1736 must have been sold to potential visitors. In commissioning views of his latest garden layouts at Chiswick, Lord Burlington had Pieter Andreas Rysbrack paint several sets of these canvases that could have hung in Burlington House, Piccadilly, and at his Yorkshire country seat, as reminders of the progress of his perfect Palladian villa and its setting. The gardens at Chiswick were also well known from a set of engravings published in 1753.

Detail of George Lambert's *View from the Cascade Terrace at Chiswick*, *c* 1742, oil on canvas (English Heritage, Chiswick House)

When George Lambert painted a fine prospect of Chiswick House and its gardens around 1742 (*see* p 41), he invested greater artistic ambition in the composition of this fine painting, which is full of the atmosphere of a late summer's evening. Lambert is traditionally claimed to be the first native-born British landscape painter. If in his view of Chiswick the foreground figures leaning on a balustrade resemble characters on a stage it may be because Lambert found steady employment as a painter of scenery for the theatre.

The Italianate summer light that filters through the leaves and garden sculpture in Lambert's view of Chiswick and also in his view of Dover Castle (*c* 1738, *see* p 45) seems to have been imported from the paintings of the 17th-century master Claude Lorrain. Richard Wilson's visit to Italy in 1750 is considered a turning point in the native school of landscape painting, as he returned with an 'educated' eye, able to see and depict England's countryside as if in old master paintings. His oblique view of Marble Hill (*c* 1762, *see* p 85) is in striking contrast to the more direct record from the opposite bank of the Thames by Augustin Heckell, published in 1749. Both are idealised but in different ways. Wilson's two visions of Okehampton Castle (*c* 1771–2; *c* 1774, *see* pp 90–1) emulate Claude Lorrain and Jacob van Ruisdael, as essays in the French-Italian and Dutch manner of old master painting.

Comparison with Hendrik Frans de Cort's view of Launceston Castle (*c* 1790, *see* p 81) confirms that the antiquarian tradition made the transition to oil painting from engravings and book illustrations. Full of topographical information, it was probably painted to hang in the seat of the owners of the uninhabitable castle, as a polite hint to their guests of their ancient lineage. John Wootton's sporting conversation piece of a hunting party stopping to admire the ruins of Rievalux Abbey (*c* 1728, *see* p 107) might have been commissioned to tempt idle house guests out into the gardens of Duncombe Park, where the ruins had recently been incorporated into the designed landscape.

When Thomas Gainsborough declined a commission to paint a view, insisting that the subject 'must be of his own Brain', he could have come to this resolution from painting the detailed topographical prospect of Landguard Fort around 1753. Encouraged by the founding of the Royal Academy of Arts in 1768 more painters shared the ambition to paint original works that might rival the old masters and raise the artist's status above that of a tradesman. John Inigo Richards, for example, worked as principal scene painter at Covent Garden and in his rather theatrical nocturnal view of Okehampton Castle he has moved on from topography to the taste for the Sublime.

The growth of recreational travel in the 1770s, particularly to the Lake District and Wales, ensured the survival of the topographical antiquarian tradition in landscape painting through commissions to illustrate books. Indeed, publishers enabled artists to

John Inigo Richards (1731–1810), *Okehampton Castle*, 1764, oil on canvas (Yale Center for British Art, Paul Mellon Collection, USA)

travel throughout Britain. The Lake District became more fashionable after the publication in 1798 of Wordsworth's *Lyrical Ballads*. Interest in north Wales grew in response to Richard Wilson's exhibited paintings of Snowdonia. The novels of Sir Walter Scott encouraged visits to the Scottish Borders; the Highlands seemed more inviting after Queen Victoria first visited Balmoral in 1848.

At first, pencil outlines with grey and blue wash proved sufficient to satisfy the market for picturesque views, as in Thomas Hearne's watercolours of Castle Acre (*c* 1771), Carlisle Castle (*c* 1777) and Furness Abbey (*c* 1777), and Michael Angelo Rooker's view of Buildwas Abbey (*c* 1790). Paul Sandby had begun his career as a military draughtsman, painting survey views of the Scottish Highlands for the Duke of Cumberland during the brutal suppression following the Jacobite Rebellion of 1745. His views of Eltham Palace would have been painted while he was principal drawing master at the Royal Military Academy in Woolwich, where he taught officers how to produce topographical watercolours. To this highly practical branch of the art Sandby brought a disciplined use of perspective, composition and silhouette that was not required of the painters for travel guides.

The creative development of watercolour as a medium for works of art of importance in their own right led to the formation in 1804 of an exhibiting body in London, the Society of Painters in Watercolours. Technical developments in the use of colour and wash took the medium further away from the grey- and blue-tinted drawings of the antiquarian tradition as ambitious artists produced finished 'exhibition watercolours'. However, as John Sell Cotman's views of Kirkham Priory (1805) and Byland Abbey (*c* 1809) show so well, as does David Cox's *Stokesay Castle and Abbey* (*c* 1820), the old familiar historic sites continued to hold their appeal into the 19th century.

The Royal Academy's Professor of Painting, Henry Fuseli (appointed 1799), had dismissed topographical views as 'the last branch of uninteresting subjects, that kind of landscape painting which is entirely occupied with the tame delineation of a given spot [of interest only to] the owners of the acres … the antiquary or the traveller'. Yet it provided many artists of ambition with a second career and must have sustained hundreds of hacks.

J M W Turner began his career around 1785 as a boy colouring engravings in a copy of Henry Boswell's *Picturesque Views of the Antiquities of England and Wales* (1776) and throughout his life he travelled to paint watercolours for publishers. Eleven examples in the following pages illustrate his growing interest in the setting of historic sites, the transitory effects of local weather and the way of life of the local people. Seeking out original viewpoints, Turner created dramatic contrasts in scale and composition, used richer colours and created his highlights by scratching and sponging out his bold washes. In this way he captured not only the special 'sense' of a place but also his own response to it and, indeed, his idea of man's place in nature in general.

John Constable's *Hadleigh Castle* (1829), along with his views of Framlingham Castle (*c* 1815), Old Sarum (1834) and Stonehenge (1836), have this same sense of tension, between making a recognisable record and expressing something far greater and less tangible: the disturbing response to the insignificance of human achievements before nature. Constable liked to present himself as the painter of the humbler landscape of his youth in Suffolk. When asked in 1822 if he had seen William Beckford's Fonthill Abbey he replied: 'I never had a desire to see sights – and a gentleman's park is my aversion. It is not beauty because it is not nature.' Yet he relied on the tradition of painting antiquarian sites when he sought to express something more than the beauty of nature.

Thomas Girtin's watercolours of Helmsley (*c* 1796), Dunstanburgh (*c* 1796) and Lindisfarne (*c* 1797) share the sense of ambition and independence in spirit that fuelled the portraits of places painted by his friend Turner. Nevertheless, in 1802, Girtin was invited by the collector Lord Elgin to accompany him to Constantinople as drawing tutor to Lady Elgin, at a salary less than half that of his Lordship's *valet de chambre*.

John Eaton Walker (fl 1854–66), *Kenilworth Castle, Past and Present*, 1854, oil on canvas (Private Collection)

in *The Illustrated London News* in 1852, both published on the occasion of the death of famous tenants. The view of Witley Court by J Wood was published in *The Illustrated London News* in 1843 to mark the arrival of Queen Adelaide as summer resident. Long before the coach-tour operators of Beverly Hills found their market, the appetite for viewing 'celebrity homes' provided artists with commissions. For example, the engraving of Marble Hill published in 1749 (*see* p 84) would have been recognised as showing the Thames-side villa of the retired mistress of King George II. The political theorist Jeremy Bentham recalled how, when a law student, he came uninvited to Kenwood, home of the Lord Chief Justice, Lord Mansfield, 'as a lover to the shrine of his mistress, in the hope that chance might throw him his way'.

Like the popular press, the development of photography in the 1830s gave renewed impetus to the making and selling of views of historic buildings. Displays of photographs at the Great Exhibition in 1851 stirred public interest in the new medium. If Benjamin Turner chose a rather conventional viewpoint for his photograph of Whitby Abbey around

Roger Fenton (1819–69), *Rievaulx Abbey*, 1854, albumen print (Victoria & Albert Museum)

Like Lady Elgin, Queen Victoria needed a tutor and William Leighton Leitch came to Osborne House to teach her and her children how to paint. The interior view of old Brodsworth Hall, painted by a tenant's daughter, is typical of the countless competent paintings by amateurs, at a time when watercolours were a necessary social accomplishment. Similar views were painted indoors at Kenwood in 1824 by the daughters of the 3rd Earl of Mansfield after he hired John Linnell to visit to copy portrait miniatures and provide instruction. The country house library would have been the centre of study where guests could browse through portfolios of watercolours, explore shelves of illustrated county histories and pocket a picturesque tour guide for the next day's excursion. If not enjoying the company of some itinerant artist who had been commissioned to paint views of the house and the estate they might lose themselves in a historical novel such as Sir Walter Scott's *Kenilworth* (1821) and imagine life among the knights of old, rather than in the damp ruins of the day.

The expansion of the popular press brought views of buildings into humbler homes, as in the illustrations of Ranger's House in *The Pictorial Times* in 1844 and of Walmer Castle

1852–4 (*see* p 126), Roger Fenton, in his 1854 view of Rievalux Abbey, showed how the medium could respond to a fresh eye unschooled in the fine art of landscape painting. Fenton recorded several Gothic abbeys and cloisters in the 1850s and 1860s for exhibition and sale. He was appointed official photographer to the British Museum in 1853 but spent much of his career as a lawyer. His exhibited photographs were recognisable in his day by their relatively large-scale, fine quality and by his careful use of compositional elements.

The rise of photography and the popular illustrated press could have made the topographical artist redundant. Some painters, inspired by John Ruskin's *Modern Painters* (1843–60), the most widely read art treatise of 19th-century England, committed themselves to the intense scrutiny of nature. The Pre-Raphaelites inspired a school of landscape painting in which the natural world, unencumbered by the theoretical filters of the Sublime, Beautiful and Picturesque, could almost reveal God. In Alfred William Hunt's view of Whitby (1878), the historic site still holds its appeal despite his fascination with the minutiae of its wider setting (*see* p 127).

By the end of the 19th century, the spread of the railways began to establish the scenic advertising poster as the natural successor to engravings and lithographs of watercolours. The 'golden age' of poster production came between the establishment of four large regionally based railway companies in 1923 and the creation of British Rail in 1947. Design flourished through competition for customers. Artists such as Fred Taylor, Tom Purvis and Edward McKnight Kauffer turned the limitations of colour lithography to dramatic effect by designing in simplified blocks of solid flat colours. Following the example of Toulouse Lautrec, William Nicholson and other artists inspired by Japanese woodcuts in the later 19th century, they appreciated how economy in design could give posters maximum impact. Competing resorts collaborated with the railway companies, particularly with the London & North Eastern Railway (LNER) and the London, Midland & Scottish (LMS) lines, to produce posters of sea, sand, coast and castles to attract holiday makers from London and the growing cities of the Midlands and the north. The railways also commissioned views of historic landmarks to hang inside carriages, beneath the luggage racks.

Travel was further facilitated by the arrival of the motor car, and the sale of petrol required posters with tempting reasons to buy more fuel: an opportunity taken up in

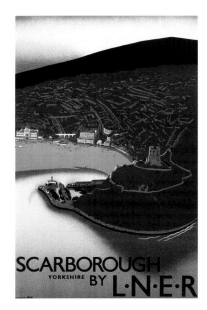

Tom Purvis (1888–1957), *Scarborough, Yorkshire by L.N.E.R.*, 1923, poster (National Railway Museum)

Edwin Byatt (1888–1948), *Rievaulx Abbey, Yorkshire*, 1937, rail carriage poster for LNER (Private Collection)

particular by Shell-Mex Ltd. In the 1930s a whole generation of graphic artists could 'Be Sure of Shell' as they designed advertisement posters to encourage drivers 'To Visit Britain's Landmarks' and 'See Britain First on Shell', such as Stonehenge by Edward McKnight Kauffer (see p 114) and Orford Castle by Allan Walton (see p 94). By implication, the Dutch company's petrol was as safe, reliable and British as our national landmarks.

The campaign began in 1932 when Shell-Mex Ltd joined British Petroleum and Eagle Oil in forming a joint marketing company. It promoted not only fuel but young British artists, such as Graham Sutherland, Ben Nicholson and Rex Whistler. Car drivers would be tempted while out on the road by artistic posters, on the sides and backs of lorries. Such mobile posters heeded the protests of the Council for the Preservation of Rural England (founded in 1926) at the spread of advertising hoardings in the countryside. In the catalogue to an exhibition of posters held at the National Gallery in 1938 the director, Kenneth Clark, described Shell-Mex and BP as 'among the best patrons of modern art … they make it possible for an artist's work to be enjoyed by a very large number of people'.

The American graphic designer Edward McKnight Kauffer was regarded as the leader of the new profession. Paul Nash wrote in 1935 that he was 'responsible above anyone for the change in attitude towards commercial art in this country'. In 1938 Kauffer himself summed up the duty of 'the artist in advertising' as to 'help to make it worthy of the civilisation that needs it'.

With two world wars in half a century, the blitzed nation found that historic sites held a strong appeal as symbols of stability, continuity, survival and national character. English artists dissatisfied with the European avant-garde and with the road to radical abstraction took renewed interest in the landscape painters of the Romantic era. A Surrealist painting like Paul Nash's response to Avebury, *Equivalents for the Megaliths* (1935), and the neo-Romanticism of John Piper's dramatic interpretations of ruins such as Binham Priory, Byland Abbey and Kirby Hall, reaffirm the significance such places held for new generations. L S Lowry's view of Clifford's Tower in the centre of York (see p 43) includes industrial cooling towers in the background beyond the recently cleared setting of urban lawn, perhaps as a gentle reminder that such ancient monuments could lose their magic once rescued and restored by the state as tourist attractions. By contrast, in Barry Martin's view of Battle Abbey at night (2004), ghosts from 1066 seem to do battle with the costumed performers of today's 'special event' re-enactment groups (see p 19). Through all the layers of public afterlife of historic buildings, artists are able to detect and capture the essential *genius loci*, the enigmatic, poetic spirit of the place.

While artists continued to be inspired by romantic ruins, the antiquarians were becoming increasingly concerned with countering the deterioration and loss of the nation's architectural landmarks. The government recognised these concerns in the late 19th century and funded professionals to make their own tours of inspection. Thanks to pioneers of conservation like William Morris, the restoration of historic buildings was now no longer left to over-zealous architects such as George Gilbert Scott and James Wyatt, dubbed 'Wyatt the destroyer' for his insensitive alterations to such national treasures as Salisbury Cathedral. In 1882 the first Ancient Monuments Protection Act created the post of Inspector of Ancient Monuments. The first Inspector, General Augustus Pitt-Rivers, was given the job of identifying 50 ancient monuments to be 'scheduled' – monitored by the Inspector and protected from developers. In 1913 the Ancient Monuments Act extended the principle of public interest in historic properties beyond monuments to include all historic buildings; 50 years later over 3,000 sites had been scheduled.

Private owners soon saw the benefits of transferring responsibility for maintenance and public access to the state through Guardianship agreements. In 1913 Pembroke College Cambridge put Framlingham Castle into state care and in 1918 Stonehenge was given to the nation. Other sites and properties soon followed, such as Whitby Abbey in 1920, Tintagel in 1929 and Kirby Hall in 1930. In 1946 the freehold of Wrest Park was purchased and in 1948 the freehold of Audley End passed to the state in lieu of death duties. This growing and diverse national collection of architecture received most additions in the 1950s when the Ministry of Defence handed over forts such as Pendennis, St Mawes and Tilbury after derequisitioning.

As the initial consolidation works were launched at each site in the inter-war years by specialists from the Ministry of Public Buildings and Works so the settings of ruins were cleared and levelled. Architectural fragments that had lain where they had fallen centuries before were excavated; with archaeology came new research and understanding of the stories buried by time and benign neglect. In these years excavations were accelerated by the supply of demobbed soldiers and of the unemployed during the Depression. The familiar setting for consolidated ruins post-excavation, of a flat expanse of perfect lawn, worthy of cricket, is perhaps the most conspicuous legacy of 20th-century conservation. The philosophical approach of 'repair as found' did not include the setting. In its lucid exposure of the footprints of lost buildings the triumphant archaeologist's tidy lawn is the equivalent of the minimalist 'white box' galleries for contemporary art favoured at that time. The very antithesis of the Romantic sensibility, the formal lawn limited the range of responses that ruins could invite and left the way clear for a well informed 'interpretation scheme'. Fortunately, artists had got there first and their views record the way the settings evolved through previous centuries of decay.

The programme of quasi-nationalisation of historic sites in the first half of the 20th century and the rediscovery of England's antiquarian past are reflected in the representations of these sites in modern paintings, illustrated travel guides and posters. The neo-Romantic images of Nash, Piper, Sutherland and others were not only a reaction to industrialisation and international Modernism: they were expressions of a pride in what had been saved through the price of war, a way of life in England that still seemed at risk. Popular interest in archaeology and architecture also reflected a democratisation of taste, as popular guides and affordable travel by car and train provided new opportunities for self-education.

The Guardianship deeds that transferred the care of sites from private owners to the state continue to be honoured today through the changing generations of freeholders. Occasionally, properties have been added to the national collection against the wishes of the owners through a Compulsory Purchase Order, as was required to save Witley Court in 1972. Battle Abbey, with the battlefield of 1066, came as a gift of the American people in 1976, to mark the bicentenary of their independence.

In 1984 the Historic Buildings and Monuments Commission, now known as English Heritage, was created and a series of acquisitions favoured historic houses with collections. In 1986, with the Abolition of the Greater London Council, the freeholds of three houses with collections were transferred to English Heritage: The Iveagh Bequest, Kenwood; Marble Hill; and Ranger's House. Brodsworth Hall was donated in 1990 following the purchase of its contents by the National Heritage Memorial Fund, and in 1995 Eltham Palace transferred from the Ministry of Defence. Charles Darwin's home, Down House, was purchased by English Heritage in 1996 with funds donated by The Wellcome Trust. Most recently, in 2004, Apsley House and the Wellington Collection passed from the Victoria & Albert Museum to English Heritage.

This national collection of architecture now has 412 historic properties open to the public and interest in visiting them seems stronger than ever. The same historic landmarks that inspired artists over the last three centuries are popular again today, and the government is committed to investing in their preservation and promotion.

Successive governments have come to admire and value historic sites in different ways. When the Historic Buildings and Monuments Commission was created in 1984 by Margaret Thatcher's government, the country's manufacturing industries were in decline

Fred Taylor (1875–1963), *Whitby. 'It's Quicker by Rail'*, 1923, poster for LNER (National Railway Museum)

John Piper (1903–92), *Stonehenge*, 1981, screenprint (Private Collection)

and the economy was becoming more reliant on tourism. Britain is now the world's fifth most popular tourist destination, in spite of being the one with the worst weather. Investment in improving the appeal of historic landmarks has been a means of attracting income from both foreign and domestic visitors. The Labour Party government has continued to enhance English Heritage's portfolio but with a different role for historic landmarks as symbols of regional and national identity. The sites are now also expected to play an important role in stimulating local pride and encouraging community interest in the historic roots of their region. As post-colonial Britain comes to terms with itself as a multi-racial nation so these historic sites are valued as a reminder of its already diverse origins. The sites reveal the early contribution of many other cultures, including the Romans, Saxons, Vikings and Normans, and of international monastic communities such as the Cistercians. The changing role of historic sites and the varying values attached to them have much to contribute to the current debate over the meaning of 'Englishness'.

The long tradition of travelling to ancient sites and great buildings in England has many motivations, from spiritual quest to artistic creativity. The images selected for this book are but a tiny fraction of the many that these special places have inspired. As some of the more contemporary paintings and drawings confirm, England's historic sites will continue to inspire new generations, so long as they are conserved and cherished.

George Robertson (1749–88), *A View of Kenwood*, 1780, grey wash, pen and pencil
(English Heritage, Kenwood)

THE SITES

Apsley House, London

THE FIRST DUKE OF WELLINGTON (1769–1852) purchased Apsley House in 1817, two years after he defeated Napoleon at the Battle of Waterloo on 18 June 1815. The most conspicuous house in London after Buckingham Palace, it overlooks Hyde Park Corner and was known as 'No 1 London' as it stood at the toll gates marking the western entrance to the capital. These two early views of Apsley House were painted on Meissen porcelain dessert plates about 1818 as part of a dining service presented to Wellington by King Frederick Augustus IV of Saxony. They show just how busy Hyde Park could be, with Piccadilly filled with carriages, promenaders strolling through Green Park and troops marching by. Robert Adam built the house between 1771 and 1779 for Henry Bathurst, 1st Baron Apsley. The plates record its appearance before Wellington employed Benjamin Dean Wyatt to remodel the house between 1819 and 1830.

Wellington lived at Apsley House for 35 years, from the age of 48 until he died at Walmer Castle in Kent (*see* p 122) aged 83. From this palatial town house he pursued a second, less successful, career as a statesman and endeavoured to live up to public expectations of Britain's greatest military hero. Wellington served as Prime Minister from 1828 to 1830, but his popularity sank to its lowest point in 1831 when the windows of Apsley House were broken by rioters. The iron shutters and high railings he installed may be the origin of the familiar term 'The Iron Duke'.

Wellington filled Apsley House with nearly 3,000 paintings, sculptures and works of art made of silver, silver gilt and porcelain, together with military trophies such as swords, batons and medals. Visitors in his own lifetime felt it looked more like a museum than his home. With the many portraits of Napoleon and his family, generals and politicians, there is a sense of Wellington collecting in order to consolidate his reputation, knowing that Waterloo was 'the nearest run thing you ever saw in your life'. The greatest masterpieces in the collection are the paintings by Diego Velazquez, Bartolme Esteban Murillo, Jusepe de Ribera and Peter Paul Rubens and other works formerly belonging to the Spanish royal family that had been taken by Napoleon's brother Joseph before he fled the country as the defeated King of Spain. Wellington's cavalry intercepted Joseph Bonaparte's baggage and

found the paintings. He added The Waterloo Gallery to Apsley House to display the finest of 165 paintings from the Spanish Royal Collection that he was allowed to keep. Here he held the annual Waterloo Banquet in tribute to his fellow veterans and hosted almost regal receptions, for he also held the Belgian title Prince of Waterloo.

Given the celebrity of the Duke and the prominent location of his London home, Apsley House has been the subject of almost innumerable engraved views. The finest prints record the spectacle of Wellington's funeral on 18 November 1852, by which time his reputation had recovered and the nation mourned.

After Louis Hague (1806–85), *Funeral of the Duke of Wellington, The Funeral Car Passing the Archway at Apsley House, November 18th 1852*, 1853, engraving (Guildhall Library, London)

Above left: *Apsley House from Hyde Park, c* 1818, Meissen porcelain dessert plate (Wellington Collection, Apsley House)

Above right: *Apsley House from Hyde Park Corner, c* 1818, Meissen porcelain dessert plate (Wellington Collection, Apsley House)

Audley End, Essex

AUDLEY END is named after Sir Thomas Audley, Lord Chancellor of England under Henry VIII, who was rewarded by his king with the estate of the suppressed Benedictine priory of Walden. Audley's daughter and heir, Margaret, married Thomas Howard, 4th Duke of Norfolk. Their son, Thomas, inherited the estate in 1582. He built Audley End between 1603 and 1614 after a successful naval career, which was recognised by Elizabeth I with a knighthood for his command of the *Golden Lion* against the Spanish Armada. He was later created Earl of Suffolk by James I, who also appointed him Lord High Treasurer of England (equivalent to that of Prime Minister today). His construction of this grand house was motivated by his desire for royal patronage and a formal visit from King James I, a visit that never materialised. James I is said to have remarked that Audley End seemed too great for a King but that it might do for a Lord High Treasurer. In scale it almost rivalled Hampton Court Palace.

At the beginning of the 18th century the 6th Earl of Suffolk, Henry Howard, demolished much of the house on the advice of the architect John Vanbrugh. Lady Portsmouth purchased Audley End in 1751 and in 1762 she left it to her nephew, Sir John Griffin Griffin. He spent the next 30 years and £100,000 renewing the house, commissioning Robert Adam to create a fashionable reception suite in the neoclassical taste and Lancelot 'Capability' Brown to remodel the gardens, in anticipation of a visit from George III, who never came. Ennobled as 1st Baron Braybrooke, Griffin Griffin formed an important collection of paintings, including portraits of his ancestors, as he sought to establish the house as his family seat.

This charming naïve painting by an unknown artist presents Audley End as an earthly paradise, complete with long-horned cattle. The scene is admired by a couple travelling on the London to Cambridge road in a sporty carriage, a 'Highflyer' phaeton, the kind made fashionable in the 1790s by the Prince of Wales. Another couple, strolling with their dog by the lake formed from the River Cam, notice a passing picturesque sailboat. Alongside the house is the new kitchen block, dairy and brewhouse, which Robert Adam added between *c* 1762 and 1787. Indeed, the painting may be dated to before 1784 when the laundry was built between the kitchen and brewhouse blocks. The relative prominence of these buildings, which are shown out of scale, suggests that the artist knew them. Katherine (1747–1809), second wife of Lord Braybrooke, was possibly the patron of this painting, or even painted it herself. The ornamental dairy was built for Lady Braybrooke and it was the only one of the new service buildings not screened by trees.

In contrast William Tomkins's earlier view is a more formal record. One of a set of six views of the house and estate that was painted for Lord Braybrooke, it records extensive changes made in expectation of the king's visit in 1786. Tomkins was a leading specialist painter of views of gentlemen's family seats and parks.

Much of the romantic antiquarian character of Audley End today is the creation of Richard Neville, 3rd Baron Braybrooke, who sought to restore the Jacobean ambience after he inherited the house in 1825. A scholar, he edited the first publication of Samuel Pepys' diaries and wrote *The History of Audley End and Saffron Walden* (1836). The ensemble of 36 Dutch and Italian paintings that he arranged in the new Drawing Room is one of the best preserved and documented historic hangs of paintings in Britain.

Above: Unknown artist, *Audley End*, *c* 1782, oil on canvas (Private Collection)

Left: William Tomkins (*c* 1732–92), *Audley End from
the South West*, 1788, oil on canvas (English Heritage,
Audley End)

Avebury, Wiltshire

WHEN THE ARTIST PAUL NASH first visited Avebury in 1933 he was amazed by the scale of Silbury Hill and by the ancient circle of megaliths, the great glacial boulders that had been dragged from the Downs in prehistoric times. He wrote 'monoliths stand up, sixteen feet high, miraculously patterned with black and orange lichen, remnants of the avenue of stones which led to the Great Circle. A mile away, a green pyramid casts a giant shadow.' The year before he illustrated new editions of two treatises by the 17th-century philosopher Sir Thomas Browne, in which ancient burial customs and abstract geometrical forms in nature are discussed in mystical terms. The 'X' in a circle, which Browne cites as Plato's symbol of the soul, can be seen in Nash's response to Avebury, *Equivalents for the Megaliths*. Here Nash links concerns of the Surrealist movement in the inter-war years, particularly his admiration for the art of Georgio de Chirico, to the English Romantic tradition of landscape painting.

As David Inshaw's painting of Silbury Hill attests, the mystery of the great pyramid of earth is no less powerful today. He once described the Wiltshire countryside as 'soft, curvy and round – it has a lot of feminine attributes'. He regards landscape painting as 'part of the imagination of the artist – a moment that the artist saw'. It is this sense of that first moment of amazement before Silbury Hill that he captures here.

The World Heritage Site at Avebury is one of the most complete prehistoric complexes in Europe. Best known for the prehistoric stone circle, which is over 4,000 years old, it also features ancient barrows, avenues and ceremonial sites spread over several miles. Many of the huge stones of the circle itself were buried in the early 14th century and this destruction of the site took place under the influence of the medieval church. The rediscovery of Avebury

'began' in 1649 when the antiquary John Aubrey came upon it while hunting. In 1663 Aubrey brought Charles II to see Avebury and the king commanded him to dig for bones. Instead, Aubrey recorded the site for his (unpublished) *Monumenta Britannica* and wrote of it as the premier site of prehistoric Britain, one that 'does as much exceed in greatness the so reknowned Stonehenge, as a cathedral doeth a parish church'. Aubrey encouraged interest in the ancient Britons who 'were two or three degrees I suppose, less savage than the Americans'.

Between 1719 and 1724 the best-known English antiquary, William Stukeley, made his own records of the site. Since Aubrey's discovery, the village had expanded and the well-preserved stones had been broken up and dragged away for use by local builders and to clear fields for farming. Stukeley traced the vast stones in the fabric of village houses and field walls. He was horrified by 'the barbarous massacre of stone here' but surveyed and measured for the day 'when the Country finds an advantage in preserving its poor reliques'. His account *Abury: A Temple of the British Druids* (1743) is illustrated with his engraved views of megaliths in fenced fields. Archaeological research continued in the 19th century when theorists competed to explain Avebury as a temple, burial ground or astronomical calendar.

The appearance of Avebury today is largely the work of an heir to a marmalade fortune.

Alexander Keiller purchased Avebury Circle, the West Kennet Avenue, the manor and farm in 1934 and began excavations. Keiller raised and reset many of the stones at this time. Archaeological finds are now stored and displayed at the Alexander Keiller Museum. Responsibility for Avebury is shared between English Heritage and the National Trust.

Far left: David Inshaw (b 1943), *Silbury Hill*, 1989, oil on canvas (Private Collection)

Near left: William Stukeley (1687–1765), *A Prospect of Abury Steeple*, 1740, engraving (Private Collection)

Above: Paul Nash (1889–1946), *Equivalents for the Megaliths*, 1935, oil on canvas (Tate Collections)

Battle Abbey, East Sussex

ARRY MARTIN'S MYSTERIOUS NOCTURNAL EVOCATION of Battle Abbey and the battlefield of 1066 seems to be lit by a lightning flash. His large drawing, specially commissioned for this book, is over a metre wide. Executed in Martin's distinctive attacking style the charcoal captures the spirit of the place where Norman knights, court jesters and medieval monks can still be encountered today, if only in historical re-enactments. In contrast, J M W Turner's watercolour shows the open field spread serene before the abbey and town of Battle, the only allusion to the historic conflict coming from the foreground detail of a boy pelting a snake with stones.

William the Conqueror defeated King Harold at the Battle of Hastings on 14 October 1066. The events are best known from the Bayeux Tapestry, which was made in the south of England before 1082. In 1476 it is recorded in the cathedral in Bayeux, Normandy and today it can be seen in a museum in the town. On 25 December the conqueror was crowned King William I in Westminster Abbey. To this day William's victory remains the last successful invasion of the British Isles.

The Benedictine abbey at Battle was founded in 1070, the year William was recrowned by papal legates. Tradition holds that William founded the abbey to keep a vow made before the battle. However, this legend has been traced to a forged charter produced by the monks in 1154 to persuade King Henry II to grant them exemption from the control of the Bishop of Chichester. It seems more likely that William founded the abbey to please the papal authorities and to fill the gap he had found in the nation's defences, without going to the expense of establishing a fully defended castle. The first monks were imported from the Benedictine abbey of Marmoutier on the Loire. The 14th-century gatehouse provided a magnificent fortified entrance and remains intact.

With the Dissolution of the monasteries, Henry VIII gave the abbey and much of its estate in 1538 to Sir Anthony Browne, his Master of the Horse. Browne demolished the church, chapter house and part of the cloisters and then converted the west range into his private residence. His descendants sold the estate in 1715 to Sir Thomas Webster. It remained the property of his descendants until 1976 when, to mark the bicentenary of the United States of America, a group of American citizens donated funds for the purchase of the abbey and battlefield for the nation. Battle Abbey School has occupied the site of the abbot's lodgings since the 1920s.

The abbot's great hall is open to visitors during the school holidays and contains one of the largest paintings on canvas in Britain. Measuring over 5 by 9 metres, it depicts Sir Godfrey Webster as William the Conqueror and was painted around 1820 by Frank W Wilkin. Removed in 1862, it was rediscovered wrapped around a flagpole in store in Hastings and has recently been restored and reinstated by English Heritage's team of paintings conservators.

J M W Turner (1775–1851), *Battle Abbey*, 1816, watercolour (Private Collection)

Barry Martin (b 1943), *Battle Abbey*, 2004, charcoal (Collection of the artist)

Berwick-upon-Tweed, Northumberland

THE BUCK BROTHERS' PANORAMIC PROSPECT OF BERWICK seems serene yet it was produced when the town stood on the front line of England's defences against a Scottish invasion. Berwick is here seen from the south, from the secure English bank of the River Tweed, in a view drawn for engraving. The rather idyllic sense of calm would have reassured English buyers of the prints, particularly after war with France in 1744 and the Scottish Jacobite invasion led by Prince Charles Stewart in 1745.

Berwick stands near the border between Scotland and England, on the north bank of the River Tweed, and was once one of Europe's most fortified towns. After 300 years of disputed control Berwick officially became part of England in 1482, but it only became 'English' at the end of the 16th century when James VI of Scotland was accepted as the future king of England.

The 12th-century castle at Berwick was captured and rebuilt by Edward I in 1296. In 1530 the Master of Ordnance to Henry VIII came in person to supervise 300 men repairing and upgrading the two miles of walls and bulwarks, ready for an invasion of French and Scottish forces. In 1547 20,000 men were mustered at Berwick. The 16th-century town fortifications survive almost in their entirety and the artillery defences, begun in 1558, are among the best to survive anywhere. These ramparts and earthworks became the most costly investment by the government of Elizabeth I. By the end of the

16th century £250,000 had been spent on fortifying this frontier harbour town. The walls were last repaired after the Jacobite Rebellion of 1745.

In medieval times soldiers were billeted in the homes of the townspeople, but permanent accommodation for soldiers was constructed in Berwick after the Jacobite Rebellion of 1715. The earliest design, from 1717, has been attributed to Nicholas Hawksmoor. The parade ground and barracks, built 1717–21, remained in military use by the King's Own Scottish Borderers until 1964 and survive intact today.

J M W Turner's engraving of Berwick, from his earlier watercolour, presents the old castle and bridge silhouetted against the River Tweed with the North Sea beyond. It was engraved in 1833 as the frontispiece to Sir Walter Scott's *Poetical Works* (1834). Turner had first met Scott in 1818 when he went to Edinburgh to discuss illustrations for the writer's *Provincial Antiquities of Scotland*. Turner visited Berwick to paint his watercolour on 10 August 1831, when he was staying at Scott's home, Abbotsford House, and was making sketching trips in the Borders.

The popularity of Berwick grew rapidly in the 1840s among English sightseers en route to Scotland following the creation of Robert Stephenson's North British Railway with its picturesque coastal route. Ironically, the railway's arrival at Berwick necessitated the demolition of the castle.

Samuel Buck (1696–1779) and Nathaniel Buck (fl 1727–53), *The South View of Berwick Upon Tweed*, c 1743–5, pen, ink and wash on paper (Yale Center for British Art, Paul Mellon Collection, USA)

After J M W Turner (1775–1851), *Berwick-on-Tweed*, 1833, engraving (Tate Collections)

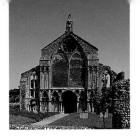

Binham Priory, Norfolk

A GREATER CONTRAST between the Buck brothers' topographical depiction of Binham Priory and John Piper's dramatic evocation of the ruins at night would be difficult to imagine. The frontal viewpoint and shallow foreground setting give Piper's composition a theatrical air, like an empty stage lit through stained glass. The rich use of colour and tonal contrast also sets his vision in the Romantic tradition of the Gothic Revival and the Sublime. Piper worked as an author, illustrator, muralist and stage designer. His commissions included stained glass windows for Coventry Cathedral and scenery and costumes for opera at Covent Garden. But he is best known for such allusive watercolours and prints of churches, castles and country houses in England and Wales. His views of Byland Abbey, Framlingham Castle, Kirby Hall, Stokesay Castle and Stonehenge are also illustrated in this book.

Piper's vision of rural buildings is indebted to the Romantic revival in landscape painting of the inter-war years of 20th-century England. More specifically, they follow the rediscovery of the mystical landscapes of Samuel Palmer by Graham Sutherland and by other artists following an exhibition of Palmer's drawings, etchings and woodcuts at the Victoria & Albert Museum in 1926. To the English neo-Romantics, the 18th century's discovery of landscape, antiquities and architecture provided an alternative path to modernism. As Piper once explained, he needed 'to find something to replace the object that Cubism destroyed'. Like John and Paul Nash, Piper contributed to the series of *Shell Guides to Great Britain* edited by John Betjeman that did so much to popularise the connoisseurship of rural architecture in the 1930s as motor cars became more widely available.

The Benedictine priory at Binham was founded around 1103 by Pierre de Valoines, a nephew of William the Conqueror. Despite being purchased at the Dissolution of the monasteries for use as a family home, Binham was abandoned and stripped for building materials. Today the west end of the nave survives as the local parish church, amid extensive ruins. The west front's fine windows were bricked up for structural reasons in the early 19th century when much of the church was demolished. The historic church fittings include part of a painted rood screen and a 15th-century font carved with panels representing the Seven Sacraments.

Samuel Buck (1696–1779) and Nathaniel Buck (fl 1727–53), *The South West View of Binham Priory in the County of Norfolk*, 1738, engraving (English Heritage)

John Piper (1903–92), *Binham Abbey*, 1981, screenprint (Private Collection)

Bolsover Castle, Derbyshire

HIGH ON A RIDGE ABOVE THE ROLLING HILLS OF DERBYSHIRE, Bolsover Castle is a magical survivor from the 16th century. Here in 1634, King Charles I and his queen, Henrietta Maria, were entertained with a masque specially written for them by Ben Jonson. With feasts and dancing, the entertainment cost nearly £15,000; the king's host, William Cavendish, was left 'plunged in debt'. Built on the site of a 12th-century castle, Bolsover was a romantic picturesque folly rather than a fortified home. Designed by Robert Smithson and his son John and grandson Huntingdon, this fairy-tale castle was built for Sir Charles Cavendish from 1612 and completed by his son William in the 1660s.

The son of Bess of Hardwick and her second husband, William Cavendish, Sir Charles Cavendish had lived at Chatsworth as a child. His choice of location for his Jacobean castle afforded him commanding prospects towards Chatsworth, Hardwick Hall, Sutton Hall (now Sutton Scarsdale), Worksop Manor and other fine homes; it also ensured that his neighbours could not overlook his little fantasy.

The most conspicuous feature from the valley below, the Little Castle may resemble a Norman keep but, with its turrets and battlements, it was conceived as theatrical scenery. This petite house of pleasure for chivalric courtiers provided guests with suites of rooms decorated with allegorical paintings. A sculpture of Hercules presides over the entrance and the symbolic paintings invited Cavendish's guests to follow his 'Labours' up to the Elysium and Heaven rooms. From here they could look down into the enclosed Fountain Garden and find further inspiration in its statue of Venus, goddess of love.

The Riding House range was built in the 1630s by William Cavendish to stable his 54 horses. A master of horsemanship, he published the classic book of instruction in dressage, *La Méthode Nouvelle et Invention Extraordinaire de Dresser les Chevaux* (1658), which was illustrated with engravings that show Bolsover in the background. In the 1630s he enlarged Bolsover with the addition of the Terrace Range, containing a suite of state rooms, in the hope of inviting the king and being appointed Master of the Horse, a position he never attained.

Tourists were visiting the abandoned castle by 1789 when one James Byng noted in his diary that it would be suitable as a school 'which shou'd always be done with these old houses'. The local curate moved into the Little Castle in 1828 and filled the Star Chamber with a collection of relics of Mary, Queen of Scots and the Stuart princes. A serialised novel in *The British Churchman* about William Cavendish's royal cousin, Arbella Stuart, had the heroine sitting in the same room listening to 'the genii of Bolsover, in the wild and fitful blasts, which do reign in this castle'. Engravings of the castle in magazines and antiquarian publications such as Joseph Nash's *Mansions of England in the Olden Time* (1839–49) further contributed to Bolsover's appeal to Victorian sightseers. This set of four watercolours is animated by several groups of admirers in summer dress; the views may have been painted for engraving in aquatint.

Engraving from *General System of Horsemanship* (1658) by William Cavendish, 1st Duke of Newcastle (1593–1676), showing Bolsover's Little Castle in the background

English School (possibly John Charles Buckler (1770–1851)), *Bolsover Castle*, early 19th century, watercolours (English Heritage)

Boscobel and White Ladies Priory, Shropshire

COMMISSIONED BY KING CHARLES II, Robert Streeter's double portrait of houses in a forest also includes, on the far right, a distinctive old oak tree. The painting would have been the focus of the king's favourite story: his escape after defeat at the Battle of Worcester on 3 September 1651. The most famous tree in Britain – the 'Royal Oak' at Boscobel – has been attracting tourists since the middle of the 17th century. Antiquarian merchandise such as snuff boxes and toys were fashioned from its wood; it also appears in engravings, books and on decorated dishes. Standing in a farmed field by a timber-framed hunting lodge, the original tree found fame when it sheltered Charles II from Oliver Cromwell's search party.

Defeated at the Battle of Worcester on 3 September 1651, the 20-year-old son of Charles I had initially sought refuge at a nearby house, White Ladies, at dawn the next day. There he disguised himself as a servant, cutting his hair short and darkening his face with soot. Setting off for Wales he soon turned back and hid in the tree all day on Saturday 6 September, while Cromwell's army searched below. At night he slept at Boscobel, just 137 metres away, in a secret space that had probably been constructed to hide Catholic priests. On Sunday evening Charles made his escape, eventually sailing for France. There he remained in exile until the Restoration of the monarchy in 1660.

Much is known as the romantic tale became celebrated and accounts appeared within months. Thomas Blount's *Boscobel, or the History of His Sacred Majesty's Most Miraculous Preservation* (1660) included an engraving of the two houses in the forest by Wenceslaus Hollar. In 1680 the king dictated his own version of his escape to the diarist Samuel Pepys but it was not published until 1766.

Tourism increased after Sir Walter Scott included a fictionalised account of the Boscobel episode in his historic novel *Woodstock* (1826). Another popular retelling *Boscobel or the Royal Oak* (1872) by William Harrison Ainsworth, first appeared in the *New Monthly Magazine*. The tree's destruction by tourists, who stripped the boughs and bark for souvenirs, prompted the building of a protective wall by 1680. In 1706 John Evelyn recorded the oak's death; six years later William Stukeley noted a younger tree growing nearby, which is probably the 'Royal Oak' we admire today.

Boscobel had been built as a small woodland hunting lodge by the eldest son of the owner of White Ladies, using the picturesque local vernacular style. The name derives from the Italian for beautiful forest, *bosco bello*. Tenant farmers showed the embowered house to curious strangers. Restoration of the house began in 1812 and rooms were filled with a new collection of 17th-century furniture and objects. The first guidebook appeared in the mid-19th century and regular opening hours were introduced by 1870.

White Ladies was demolished in the 18th century (leaving only the remains of a nunnery's medieval church) and Boscobel was much enlarged in the 19th century.

Wenceslaus Hollar (1607–77), *Boscobel*, 1660, engraving published in Thomas Blount's *Boscobel, or the History of his Sacred Majesty's Most Miraculous Preservation* (1660)

Fortunately the painting by Streeter, the king's Sergeant Painter, records both houses, which in fact stood miles apart. Boscobel is shown in its original form on the right, before the exposed timber framing was covered with stucco. The painting also shows Charles II escaping from the back of White Ladies while the rest of his supporters leave from the front. Commissioned by Charles II around 1670 to commemorate his adventure, it was recorded in the collection of his younger brother, James II, and remains in the Royal Collection at Hampton Court today. Streeter's view of Boscobel is an early example of the country house portrait, a genre of topographical landscape painting that became popular in the following century.

Robert Streeter (1621–79), *Boscobel House and White Ladies*, *c* 1670, oil on canvas (Royal Collection, Hampton Court)

Brodsworth Hall, South Yorkshire

BRODSWORTH HALL was but a sparkle in its architect's eye when this watercolour was painted to seduce a client into commissioning construction. Most architects' presentation drawings exceed the completed buildings in ambition and cost but Brodsworth Hall stands today with only minor differences. This was thanks not only to the wealth of the first owner but also to the family's other interests.

When Peter Thellusson, a third generation banker of Huguenot descent, died in 1797 leaving some £700,000 his will caused a national sensation. His father, Isaac, had served as Genevan ambassador in Paris and on his death in 1755 he left a fortune and an art collection. About five years later Peter moved to London, married into a Lincolnshire landowning family and bought the Brodsworth estates. After his death, his will revealed that he had left most of his wealth (tens of millions of pounds at today's values) in trust to accumulate for three generations. On the death of his last great-grandson it was to be divided between his 'eldest male lineal descendants' or, if none survived, be used to pay off the National Debt.

His family challenged the terms of the banker's legacy and litigation continued for many years, but the courts upheld Thellusson's will, despite fears for the eventual impact of such a private fortune on the nation's economy. In 1880 Parliament passed the Accumulations Act (the 'Thellusson Act' as it is known) to limit the time over which property may accumulate. In Charles Dickens's novel *Bleak House* (1852) the interminable suit of Jarndyce versus Jarndyce, which drags on through generations, is thought to have been inspired by the Thellusson case, among others. In the novel, by the time the case is finally settled, all the inheritance had been spent on lawyers' fees. There must have been equal speculation in 1856 when the last of Thellusson's grandsons died and, three years later, the courts divided the fortune between two of his great-grandsons.

Charles Sabine Augustus Thellusson (1822–85) inherited the Brodsworth estates in 1859 and immediately demolished the 18th-century house to build a more comfortable, fashionable home. Given the fame of the family fortunes there must have been great expectations of a palatial residence, but the total cost when the house was finished and furnished was under £50,000. The new Brodsworth Hall was designed and built by a minor architect, Philip Wilkinson of London, between 1861 and 1863.

Some furniture and paintings were brought from the old family home. A watercolour by Anna Louisa Flint, the daughter of a tenant of the old house, painted around 1830, records in romantic disarray a corner of the room of the amateur artist (it is inscribed 'The Artist's Boudoir') at the time when the house and family fortunes were in trust under the terms of the will.

Brodsworth descended to the great-granddaughter of Charles Sabine Augustus Thellusson, Pamela Williams, who presented the house and gardens to English Heritage in 1990. Described at the time by Mark Girouard in *Country Life* as 'the most complete surviving example of a Victorian country house in England', Brodsworth Hall was found to contain over 17,000 objects. Unlike Witley Court or Wrest Park (*see* pp 128 and 130), where the classic tale of the death of the English country house can be told, Brodsworth was a determined survivor.

Recent research has revealed extensive documentation of life 'below stairs', from the accommodation and careers of servants to weddings between staff and their lives beyond domestic service. The gradual decline in numbers from 17 indoor staff to just one servant in the 1980s, holding everything together for one lady (Mrs Grant-Dalton, the mother of the donor) is the story the house tells today. Research has also uncovered an extensive collection of photographs, which, with albums and prints subsequently donated by the descendants of the owners and staff, totals 5,000 images from the 1860s to the 1980s. The photographs reveal why the house seems modest compared to more celebrated Victorian architectural extravaganzas. The builder of Brodsworth Hall spent as much again of his fortune on schooners (including the 380-ton racing yacht *Bodicea*, the largest ever built in Britain). Victorian and Edwardian society life carried on far beyond London and the country house.

Above: Attributed to Philip Wilkinson (1825/6–1905), *Design for Brodsworth Hall*, *c* 1861, watercolour (English Heritage, Brodsworth Hall)

Left: Anna Louisa Flint (b 1813), *The Artist's Boudoir, Brodsworth Hall*, *c* 1830, pencil and watercolour (English Heritage, Brodsworth Hall)

Buildwas Abbey, Shropshire

THE MONASTERY AT BUILDWAS was founded in 1135 by the Savigniac order; 12 years later they merged with the Cistercians who completed the building by 1200. Income for the abbey came partly from tolls from a bridge across the River Severn. Close to England's frontier with Wales, the abbey lay in the path of military action. In 1350 Welsh soldiers took the abbot hostage and demanded a ransom. Architecturally, Buildwas is a remarkable survivor. With nearly all its church walls still standing tall it attracted artists in the 18th and 19th centuries.

In Michael Angelo Rooker's view of Buildwas Abbey the massive architecture of the nave fills the image, almost overwhelming the viewer. Rooker's rather claustrophobic fascination with the textures of stacked and sculpted stone is relieved by a group of gypsies waiting for their dinner as it cooks in a pot hung from a tripod of branches. For this group, and the goats, Rooker would have turned to his collection of engravings after Dutch masters, such as Nicholaes Berchem, Hendrik Hondius and Paulus Potter. For the architectural composition he seems to have been looking at G B Piranesi's dramatic engravings of ancient Rome's remains. The care Rooker has taken to animate the abbey with characters reflects his employment as scene-painter at the Theatre Royal, Haymarket in London and at the private theatre at Blenheim Palace. By contrast, in John Sell Cotman's view, the artist's sense of humour may be drawing a parallel between the profile of the nave, which is softened by vegetation, and that of a donkey in the foreground.

John Sell Cotman (1782–1842), *Buildwas Abbey*, c 1810, watercolour on paper (Leeds Museums and Galleries)

Michael Angelo Rooker (1746–1801), *Buildwas Abbey*, c 1790, watercolour (Whitworth Art Gallery, University of Manchester)

Byland Abbey, North Yorkshire

IN JOHN SELL COTMAN'S WATERCOLOUR the clear sharp silhouette of the west end of Byland Abbey rises against a sea of soft dark foliage, the façade balanced compositionally by a similarly skeletal tree. Cotman had a gift for seeing the flat pictorial patterns in architecture and nature. His instinct suited the medium of watercolour, which requires the patient artist to paint in stages, allowing each area of colour to dry. This was Cotman's method of teaching the medium and this view was painted some three years after he opened his 'School for Drawing and Design' in Norwich. Known as 'the English Piranesi', Cotman contributed to the popular connoisseurship of old buildings through his publications *Architectural Antiquities of Norfolk* (a collection of 400 etchings issued to subscribers in series between 1812 and 1818) and *Architectural Antiquities of Normandy* (1822). In the 20th century the sense of structure and avoidance of unnecessary details in Cotman's work appealed to the era's pursuit of abstraction in art and simplification in design. John Piper's rather theatrical view, from 1940, has similar artistic ambitions but the ruins seem to tremble beneath the threatening skies of the Second World War.

Originally the nave at Byland must have presented a colourful spectacle when the sun shone through the stained glass of the great west window, down onto the green and yellow glazed floor tiles. The stained glass is long gone and only the supporting arc of the great round rose window remains, but many of the tiles are still *in situ*, while others are in the site museum and in the British Museum.

As at Buildwas, the abbey was founded by monks of the Savigniac order in 1134; 13 years later they too joined with the Cistercians. The abbey church was completed in 1225 and is noted for its fine carved capitals and corbels, now on display in the site museum. King Edward II dined at Byland with the abbot in 1322, just before the Scots pillaged the abbey.

With the Dissolution of the monasteries (1536–40) paving tiles were often left undisturbed when monasteries were abandoned. Byland is the only example in the world of large expanses of 13th- to 15th-century mosaic flooring still in its original setting. The technique of inserting white clay into an impressed design, followed by glazing and firing, had been used in France around 1200. Medieval ruins of this kind attracted not only artists and antiquarians. At Fountains Abbey in 1863 the tiles were studied by tile manufacturers from Coalbrookdale, Shropshire.

John Piper (1903–92), *Byland Abbey*, 1940, screenprint (Private Collection)

John Sell Cotman (1782–1842), *Byland Abbey*, *c* 1809, watercolour (Norwich Castle Museum)

Carisbrooke Castle, Isle of Wight

THE VAST UNBROKEN SKIES OF THE ISLE OF WIGHT have caught the artist's interest in this prospect of Carisbrooke Castle seen from a low viewpoint. Painted in blue tonal washes over ink (the customary technique of the late 18th century, as favoured by Paul Sandby and Thomas Hearne), Joseph Charles Barrow has included members of the garrison at ease, three years into the war with France.

William the Conqueror understood the strategic importance of the Isle of Wight as a base from which to launch an invasion of the English mainland and he realised that whoever held Carisbrooke held the whole island. Therefore, after his successful conquest, he gave the Saxon fort to a kinsman, who built the first Norman castle on the site. Later fortified against the French and the Spanish, the castle was given its gatehouse in 1335 and earthwork artillery defences were added in the 1590s.

King Charles I fled to Carisbrooke in 1647, seeking the support of the resident governor, but instead found himself imprisoned, under Parliamentary orders. Three escapes were

planned, but Charles suffered the ignominy of getting himself stuck in the window bars as he tried to climb out of his chamber. He left Carisbrooke on 6 September 1648 and was executed in Whitehall on 30 January 1649. His daughter Elizabeth and son Henry were imprisoned here from August 1650, but the princess died of pneumonia.

The castle was maintained as a military defence until the 19th century. In 1896 Queen Victoria's youngest daughter, Princess Beatrice, succeeded her husband, Prince Henry of Battenberg, as Governor of the Isle of Wight on his death. She re-established the castle as the official residence and founded the present museum as a memorial to her husband.

Beatrice persuaded her mother to donate historic relics relating to the imprisonment of Charles I and formed a collection of objects relating to the history of the island; these now include memorabilia of the Poet Laureate Alfred, Lord Tennyson. After her death in 1944, the museum moved from the gatehouse to the great hall, which had formerly served as the governor's residence, where it remains today.

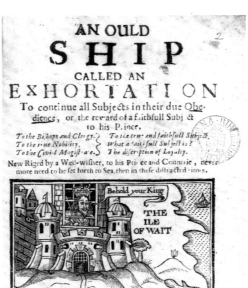

This illustrated title page from a Royalist publication of 1648 shows King Charles I imprisoned at Carisbrooke Castle (Bodleian Library, Oxford).

Joseph Charles Barrow (fl 1775–1805), *Carisbrooke Castle*, 1796, pen, ink and wash (Victoria & Albert Museum)

Carlisle Castle, Cumbria

ANNON FIRE THEIR SALUTES in Thomas Hearne's view of Carlisle Castle, with the cathedral safe in the distance. Armed and ready to repel rebels, the castle was no crumbling picturesque antiquity. When new, Hearne's image would have carried associations of the brutal suppression of the Scots, an event still within living memory after the Jacobite Rebellion of 1745.

Guarding the western end of the Anglo-Scottish border, Carlisle Castle had always been a military stronghold. The Romans maintained a garrisoned fort and town here for 300 years to protect their border against the Scots. William II came in 1092 and built a new castle following a raid. His timber castle was replaced in 1122 in stone. Fearful of a Franco-Scottish invasion, Henry VIII had the walled city and castle strengthened from 1541 to the designs of a Moravian fortress-builder, Stefan von Haschenperg, who was already employed on Henry's south coast forts.

Following their defeat at the Battle of Culloden by the 'Butcher' Duke of Cumberland, the imprisoned supporters of Bonnie Prince Charlie were led out and hanged here in 1746. In 1789 the castle was rearmed against supporters of the French Revolution at a time when Carlisle became a centre of political Radicalism. A military garrison remained until 1959. Today the castle is the headquarters of the King's Own Royal Border Regiment and is home to its regimental museum.

In 1786 the theorist of the Picturesque, William Gilpin, visited and passed his verdict, finding Carlisle 'heavy in all its parts, as these fabrics commonly are ... too perfect to afford much pleasure to the picturesque eye'. However, he felt 'hereafter, when its shattered towers and buttresses give a lightness to its parts, it may adorn some future landscape'. Despite Gilpin's verdict, Carlisle attracted painters of the picturesque. J M W Turner painted Queen Mary's Tower in 1797, recording for antiquarian interest the Tudor windows of the apartments where Mary, Queen of Scots was imprisoned in 1568 following her abdication.

In 1924 the London, Midland & Scottish Railway produced a stirring poster designed by Maurice Greiffenhagen proclaiming Carlisle to be 'The Gateway to Scotland'. With a spurred knight in shining armour on his white steed bearing the flag of St George, one would never guess that the city had ever been raided by the Scots.

Near right: J M W Turner (1775–1851), *Queen Mary's Tower, Carlisle Castle*, 1797, watercolour and grey wash (Tullie House Museum & Art Gallery)

Far right: Maurice Greiffenhagen (1862–1931), *Carlisle: The Gateway to Scotland*, 1924, poster (National Railway Museum)

LMS CARLISLE
THE GATEWAY TO SCOTLAND.
BY MAURICE GREIFFENHAGEN R.A.

Right: Thomas Hearne (1744–1817), *Carlisle Castle and Cathedral with Cannon Firing from the Castle*, c 1777, grey wash and ink (Tullie House Museum & Art Gallery)

Castle Acre Priory, Norfolk

SUNSHINE SEEMS TO WARM MASONRY to the soft texture of ripe cheese ready to crumble in this classic of the English picturesque vision. Thomas Hearne's view shows the Prior's House at Castle Acre in gentle decay, watched over only by sleepy cattle. He treats architecture as an organic mass that has swollen over time through additions and accretion. Improving with age, as the loss of stucco renders the house even more picturesque, this corner of old England at one with nature is a world away from the clean, post-conservation site created by the 20th century's archaeologists, such as Henry Rushbury presents in his railway carriage print. Hearne's watercolour was one of the first engravings issued in his *Antiquities of Great Britain* in 1778. His publication opened up the appreciation of architecture to a wider audience than the antiquarians who relied on documentary evidence, by bringing an artist's eye to the dating of architectural elements. The tradition lives on in Fred Taylor's poster for the London & North Eastern Railway, which tempts day-trippers from the suburban south-east to leave their cars at home and take the train to get close to history.

Visitor numbers were far higher at the Cluniac priory during the 14th century than they are today. Indeed, the volume of pilgrims coming to see the priory's most popular relic, the arm of St Philip, necessitated the rebuilding of the east end to give them room to rest and seek the relic's healing powers. By the 15th century Castle Acre may have been in competition with a nearby dependant house, St Andrew, Bromholm, Norfolk, which was famous for its fragment of the True Cross. In the 1490s the monks at Bromholm complained to the Pope that the monks at Castle Acre had stolen the vessels they used to celebrate mass.

Castle Acre dates from the late 11th century and takes its name from its original position within the bailey of the castle of its founder, William de Warenne. The church was built from the late 11th to the early 12th century and has a fine late Norman west end façade of blind arcades. After the Dissolution of the monasteries, the prior's lodgings next to the ruins of the church of this Cluniac priory became a private residence. An early 16th-century gatehouse of brick and flint also survives.

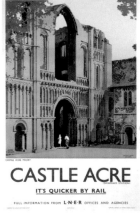

Far left: Henry Rushbury (1889–1968), *Castle Acre Priory*, 1937, print for display in railway carriages (Private Collection)

Near left: Fred Taylor (1875–1963), *Castle Acre (Swaffam Station). It's Quicker by Rail*, 1923, poster (National Railway Museum)

Thomas Hearne (1744–1817), *The Prior's House, Castle Acre, Norfolk, c* 1771, watercolour (Whitworth Art Gallery, University of Manchester)

Chiswick House, London

I N GEORGE LAMBERT'S PAINTING the low sun of a late summer evening rakes through the Italianate gardens at Chiswick House. A couple admires the fine new prospect from the balustrade above the cascade. Elegantly dressed, the gentleman wears a powdered wig and sword and his companion sports a straw bonnet to shield her eyes and fair complexion from the sun, while directing our gaze with her fan. Chiswick's creator, Richard Boyle, 3rd Earl of Burlington (1694–1753), probably commissioned this painting to hang in his country house in Yorkshire, Londesborough Hall, as a reminder of the pleasures of his villa in outer London.

Lord Burlington, Britain's greatest connoisseur, designed Chiswick House between 1727 and 1729 as a perfect villa, much like those found in ancient Rome. Inspired by the Venetian villas of Andrea Palladio (1508–80) that he had seen on his second Grand Tour, Burlington conceived this wing to his family home as a garden pavilion in which to entertain in style and enjoy his great collection of paintings, sculptures and architectural drawings, along with his library.

Having commissioned landscape painters and engravers to record his idyllic retreat he soon found his gardens filled with visitors. By 1733 admission charges were in place. Descriptions in the 1738 edition of Daniel Defoe's *A Tour thro' the Whole Island of Great Britain* and a room-by-room guide to 168 paintings in R and J Dodsley's *Environs of London* (1761) must have added to its popularity. Early engravings and drawings reveal railings immediately surrounding the house itself, presumably to keep the public at bay. John Rocque's map of the gardens, encircled by views of its architectural features and the house itself, may have been sold to potential visitors.

Burlington gradually withdrew to his family's Yorkshire seat but the paintings he commissioned convey his vision of Italy in England. In Pieter Andreas Rysbrack's view, diligent gardeners trim hedges as exotic wildfowl flutter by and the polite company make their assignations.

Pieter Andreas Rysbrack (1690–1748), *A View of Chiswick Gardens, with the Bagnio and Domed Building Alleys and the Group of Cain and Abel, c* 1729, oil on canvas (English Heritage, Chiswick House)

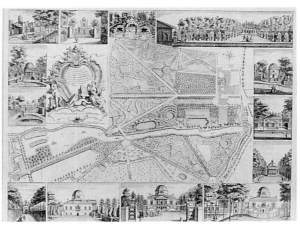

John Rocque (1704–62), *Plan of the Grounds at Chiswick*, 1736, engraving (English Heritage, Chiswick House)

George Lambert (1700–65) and possibly William Hogarth (1697–1764), *View from the Cascade Terrace at Chiswick, c* 1742, oil on canvas (English Heritage, Chiswick House)

Clifford's Tower, York

THE PAINTING BY L S LOWRY seems charming in its simplicity until one realises that this open grassy view, showing the castle and its visitors, was less than 20 years old. The prison had been demolished in 1935 and the site cleared. Lowry balances the church on the left with a cooling tower on the right. He would have been one of the tourists himself, visiting from Manchester where he was employed as a rent collector and clerk. His painting was specially commissioned by the then York City Art Gallery.

The bird's-eye view of York Castle by an unknown artist shows the cracked keep ('Clifford's Tower') standing as a feature in the private grounds of a villa; a garden wall separates it from the rest of the castle yard. Samuel Waud, the owner of the villa and tower from 1727, probably commissioned this prospect to celebrate his acquisition. Waud's guests could take a winding path up the mound to picnic and admire the views over York.

The massive artificial earth mound dates from the reign of William the Conqueror. In September 1066, east of York at Stamford Bridge, King Harold vanquished a Viking force led by the son of a Norwegian king. The next month, Harold fell at the Battle of Hastings. Recognising the threat from the north, William the Conqueror visited York in 1068 and raised the first castle there, above the River Ouse, to control access inland from the sea.

Over a century later, the timber tower on top of the mound served as a refuge for York's community of 150 Jews, who sought royal protection from a violent mob. They had grown wealthy from advancing credit to Yorkshire gentry and Cistercian abbeys such as Rievaulx. But there was no escape and the tower was burnt down on 16 March 1190 during their mass suicide; the few who preferred to surrender were murdered.

The stone keep was built between 1245 and 1272, with a gatehouse added in the 17th century. The name of the castle dates from 1596 and recognizes the Clifford family as hereditary constables. York Castle remained the royal castle in Yorkshire, providing a residence for the visiting monarch, until the Civil War (1642–51) when York fell to Parliamentary forces. In 1705 a debtor's prison, designed by William Wakefield, was built in the castle's outer bailey. The assize courts, designed by John Carr, were added in 1773–7 and the female prison, also by Carr, was built opposite in 1780. Little survives today of the castle's curtain wall and corner towers. From 1825 a vast prison was built over Waud's house and garden with a high wall around the tower.

Artist unknown, *Clifford's Tower and Samuel Waud's House*, 1730, pencil, pen, ink and wash (York Art Gallery)

L S Lowry (1887–1976), *Clifford's Tower, York*, 1952–3, oil on canvas (York Art Gallery)

Dover Castle, Kent

IN GEORGE LAMBERT'S SERENE PANORAMIC PROSPECT the open coastline and town of Dover seem safe under the castle's protection, the Union flag flying high above the ramparts, against the clouds. As in the same artist's view of Chiswick House and gardens (see p 41) the breadth of his vision may in part be due to his employment as a scene painter at Covent Garden Theatre, where he worked from 1732 until 1765. Never an abandoned romantic ruin, Dover Castle did not fire the imagination of writers of picturesque tours or of historical novels. Respected as 'the key to England' Dover has retained its strategic importance – from 1066 to the Cold War – as a military stronghold. When it appears in paintings, protecting the crest of the white cliffs of Dover, the castle invariably brings a sense of patriotic pride to coastal prospects.

The earliest rampart defences were constructed in the Iron Age. The Romans built a lighthouse and the Anglo-Saxons resettled here in the 10th century. King Harold strengthened the fortifications in 1066 to face William the Conqueror. The square keep and its surrounding walls were built in the 1180s, while the outer walls, towers and gatehouses date from the following century. Henry VIII preferred to invest in a chain of forts down at sea level (as at Walmer, Deal, Pendennis and St Mawes) where they could face French and Spanish ships. Little changed at Dover until the 18th century when, to face a Jacobite invasion, military engineers levelled the castle's skyline of towers and battlements and strengthened its platforms to suit modern artillery. Lambert's painting records the fortifications before they were further reduced during the French Revolutionary and Napoleonic Wars (1793–1815) to serve as gun emplacements.

Underground, a unique network of bomb-proof passages cut in the chalk cliffs follow the medieval example of siege tunnelling. They date from the 1790s to the 1960s. Not until 1984 did the Home Office finally abandon Dover's deepest tunnels as a potential regional seat of Government for use after a nuclear attack.

Two paintings now at Hampton Court, each about 3½ metres long, record the visit of Henry VIII to France in 1520, following the Anglo-French treaty of 1518. One painting shows his departure from England on 31 May; the companion piece records the processions, temporary palace and the spectacle of tournaments hosted by Francis I near Calais. In *The Embarkation* the view is from south-west of Dover harbour, with the castle on the left. Two forts, the Archcliff and the Black Bulwark, sound the salute. Henry VIII stands among courtiers on the deck of his ship behind the right-hand fort. In fact, artistic licence has set him on a far grander vessel than the depth of Dover harbour would have allowed.

Artist unknown, *The Embarkation of Henry VIII at Dover, c* 1550–88, oil on canvas (Royal Collection, Hampton Court)

George Lambert (1700–65), *View of Dover Castle and Bay*, *c* 1738, oil on canvas (Government Art Collection)

Down House, Kent

Above: Albert Goodwin (1845–1932), *Down House*, 1880, watercolour (English Heritage, Down House)

Right: Albert Goodwin (1845–1932), *Down House*, 1880, watercolour (English Heritage, Down House)

Left: Detail showing Charles Darwin, his wife Emma, his grandson Bernard and his dog Polly

THESE TWO WATERCOLOURS of the garden front of Charles Darwin's home, Down House, were both painted in the summer of 1880, two year's before Darwin's death. In one he can be seen seated on the veranda with his wife Emma, while their grandson Bernard looks on, with an equally patient dog, Polly. Bernard came to live at Down House following the death of his mother during childbirth in 1876.

Darwin probably invited the artist, Albert Goodwin, to visit him when he purchased his view of *The Old Hill, Winchester* after it was exhibited at the Society of Painters in Watercolours in London in 1876. It still hangs in the dining room at Down House. Goodwin had trained under the Pre-Raphaelite painter Ford Madox Brown and in 1872 John Ruskin took him to Italy as his protégé.

Darwin lived at Down House with his wife and family of 10 children in the Kent village of Downe from 1842 until he died there 40 years later. Here he researched and wrote twelve books, including *On the Origin of Species* (1859). The former vicarage became the very epicentre of scientific research and controversy in his day, attracting pilgrims of science from as far afield as North America and Russia, several of whom published accounts of their visits when they returned home. From here Darwin wrote nearly 7,000 letters, conducting his research through a world-wide web of correspondence that must make Darwin's postman one of the unsung heroes of the history of science. After Darwin's death in 1882 Down House continued to attract visitors, and his family kept his study intact as a 'shrine' for many years until the house became a girls' school. It first opened as a museum in 1929.

Today, Down House answers the advice of the great botanist Sir Joseph Hooker to Darwin's son George about 'keeping up the study and gardens for pilgrims – to make these really living evidences of your father's life and times, they should be furnished as he left them; or at any rate, as in the case of Shakespeare's house, be filled with memories of him'.

Goodwin. 80

Dunstanburgh Castle, Northumberland

THOMAS, EARL OF LANCASTER, an opponent of Edward II, built this castle from 1313, probably as a place of refuge. The extensive defensive walls enclose 11 acres and continue around the seaward side. By the beginning of the 17th century it was falling into a ruined state. The high walls made it an easy target for the latest cannon technology and it had not been repaired after a siege in the Wars of the Roses (1455–87) when Dunstanburgh, a Lancastrian stronghold, fell to the Yorkists.

The windswept silhouette of Dunstanburgh Castle rises above a treeless promontory on the rocky Northumberland shoreline. This was an ideal subject for painters of the Sublime, the mysterious and threatening alternative to the Picturesque aesthetic. In his watercolour J M W Turner fills the foreground with dark, jagged rocks that seem ready to ensnare a struggling ship. Thomas Girtin has thrown us into the water for the swirling tides and crashing waves swamp the bottom of the picture. Girtin also adds thunderous skies and lightning to enhance his view of the castle seen from far below the craggy cliffs. He sees Dunstanburgh almost as if from the hopeless viewpoint of a drowning man.

Girtin and Turner were friends and of the same age. Girtin visited Northumberland on a sketching tour for the first time in 1796 and Turner first travelled to the north of England the following year. Both launched their careers by exhibiting topographical watercolours of architectural antiquities at the Royal Academy. Girtin's early death in 1802 left Turner as the leader of the British school of Romantic landscape painting. Turner once remarked: 'If Girtin had lived, I should have starved.'

Thomas Girtin (1775–1802), *Dunstanburgh Castle in a Thunderstorm, c* 1796, watercolour (Ashmolean Museum, Oxford)

J M W Turner (1775–1851), *Dunstanburgh Castle, c* 1801–2, watercolour (Private Collection)

Eltham Palace, London

PAUL SANDBY PAINTED THE GREAT HALL AT ELTHAM around 1788. He was employed nearby in Woolwich as principal drawing master at the Royal Military Academy. The artist may have been attracted to Eltham Palace by its association with Sir Anthony van Dyck (1599–1641) who from 1635 had his summer studio here as Principal Painter to King Charles I. Van Dyck painted some of the earliest watercolours of the English landscape, probably while enjoying the Downs in North Kent. Another view of Eltham, this time from the road, was probably painted by one of Sandby's pupils, the officers who would need to record landscape and fortifications as military information. The accuracy of the steep perspective and the interest in local people suggest that it is a careful copy after a lost original by Sandby.

King Edward IV built the Hall in the 1470s as a dining hall for his court. After Westminster Hall, it is the largest of its kind in England. Eltham Palace was favoured by English monarchs as a Christmas residence from the 14th to the 16th centuries. The three surrounding parks also offered good hunting. Henry VIII was the last monarch to stay at Eltham for any length of time as Greenwich Palace proved more popular in the 16th century.

After the Civil War (1642–51) Eltham Palace was sold and the buildings on the south side of the hall were demolished. For 200 years it was used as a farm. By the time these views were painted by Sandby and his pupil, the hall had become a barn and stables. Indeed J M W Turner recorded the interiors with cattle and hay in a watercolour painted around 1793. A century later the Great Hall served as an indoor tennis court but could be seen by visitors on request.

From 1933 Stephen Courtauld, brother of the founder of the Courtauld Institute of Art, restored the hall and built a fine villa with Art Deco and eclectic interiors alongside it. The Courtaulds' house is recorded standing alongside the Hall in a view by Ethelbert White from around 1936. Within easy reach of central London, the Courtaulds' house became the 20th century's equivalent of the fashionable villas of the Georgian age, such as Marble Hill and Chiswick House, where wealthy society could entertain in style.

Circle of Paul Sandby (1730/1–1809), *The Great Hall, Eltham Palace, c* 1788, pencil and watercolour (English Heritage, Eltham Palace)

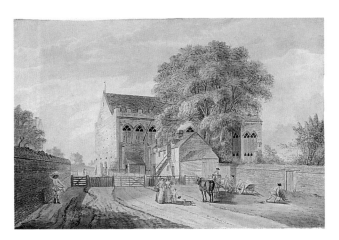

Ethelbert White (1891–1972), *The Courtaulds' Villa at Eltham Palace, c* 1936, oil on canvas (English Heritage, Eltham Palace)

Paul Sandby (1730/1–1809), *Flying a Kite near King John's Palace, Eltham*, 1788, pencil and watercolour (National Gallery of Ireland)

Fountains Abbey, North Yorkshire

IN 1768 WILLIAM AISLABIE PURCHASED THE RUINS of the greatest 12th-century Cistercian abbey in the country to provide a picturesque extension to his father's formal landscape gardens at Studley Royal. He cleared away fallen rubble, levelled the ground and rolled out turf (a tidy-minded treatment that is today associated more with the Ministry of Works' managers of historic sites in the 1930s). Aislabie also made additions to the ruins to render them yet more picturesque. The popular writer on the Picturesque, William Gilpin, criticised him in his *Observations … on the Mountains and Lakes of Cumberland and Westmoreland* (1786) for having 'pared away all the bold roughness and freedom of the scene' and given every part a 'trim polish'. Gilpin went on to threaten the current owner with the judgement of posterity:

> … he must expect a very severe prosecution in the court of Taste. The refined code of this court does not consider an elegant ruin as a man's property, on which he may exercise the irregular sallies of a wanton imagination; but as a deposit of which he is only the guardian, for the amusement and advantage of posterity. A ruin is a sacred thing.

Gilpin's notion of a national heritage was limited to the aesthetic qualities of the ruin and to a much smaller select public than Fountains Abbey welcomes today, but his sense of outrage at an owner regarding a historic building and its setting as his personal property is early evidence of a change in public attitude.

J M W Turner seems to have turned his back on the over-familiar trim ruins in his romantic evocation of an overgrown corner of the monastery at night. Turner has sought out a fresh view of the site by clambering down to the edge of the River Skell at sunset. In this ambitious watercolour, painted for exhibition at the Royal Academy when he was 23, Turner has the setting sun pour through the ruins in silhouette and through an almost tropical array of foliage and vegetation. Breaking with the topographical tradition, he presents the ruins not so much as the subject of the view as the means to express his emotional response to them. The painting is also literary in its inspiration for when Turner exhibited it at the Academy the catalogue included the following lines from James Thomson's poem *The Seasons* (1726–30):

> All ether soft'ning sober evening takes
> Her wonted station on the middle air;
> A thousand shadows at her beck –
> In circle following circle, gathers round,
> To close the face of things.

Fountains Abbey became the most admired Gothic ruin in England, rivalled only by Tintern Abbey in Monmouthshire in its awesome scale and exceptional state of preservation. Now a World Heritage Site, Fountains Abbey is maintained by English Heritage and opened to the public by the National Trust as part of the Studley Royal estate.

J M W Turner (1775–1851), *Fountains Abbey*, 1798, watercolour (York Art Gallery)

Framlingham Castle, Suffolk

THIS SKETCH IS ONE OF FOUR OPEN-AIR STUDIES of Framlingham Castle by John Constable, one of which (in the Fitzwilliam Museum, Cambridge) is dated 5 August 1815. The view illustrated here shows the castle from the north-west and includes the 16th-century moat bridge to the left and Framlingham church to the right. The angle of shadows suggest that it was made at about 5pm on the summer afternoon. In John Piper's screenprint the viewpoint is closer and lower, making the castle fill the upper half of the page, as it would appear to a besieging army.

The Norman castle at Framlingham was built by the Bigod family, Earls of Norfolk, in the 12th and 13th centuries. The design – uniform curtain walls with square towers – was the latest type of defence, in preference to the traditional keep and bailey plan. When Roger Bigod, 5th Earl of Norfolk, died in 1306, his titles and estates were forfeit to

King Edward I for refusing to fight for the king in Gascony in 1297. From 1425 John Mowbray, 2nd Duke of Norfolk, and his heirs often lived at Framlingham. During the reign of Elizabeth I it was used as a prison for priests who refused to recognise the new Church of England. The castle buildings were demolished from 1636. Only the outer curtain walls, linking 13 projecting towers, remain today.

Inside, on the site of the Norman hall, there stands a brick workhouse from 1664, a school and a poorhouse, which was built of flint in 1729. Initially intended for children, it housed 100 impoverished adults in the 18th century and only went out of use in 1839 when a new poorhouse was built in nearby Wickham Market. When Constable visited Framlingham in 1815 it would have been active as a poorhouse and not simply some picturesque abandoned ruin.

John Piper (1903–92), *Framlingham Castle*, 1971, screenprint (Tate Collections)

John Constable (1776–1837), *Framlingham Castle Viewed from the North-West*, *c* 1815, pencil (Royal Cornwall Museum, Truro)

Furness Abbey, Cumbria

IN THE PAINTING BY THOMAS SMITH OF DERBY two monks look on, one in prayer, the other in awe, as a church procession makes its way down the nave of the ruined abbey of Furness. The view may have been commissioned by the tenants of the manor house on the right, which was built around 1670. Smith was one of the first professional painters of country houses but was no great artist; he appears to have based this property portrait on an engraving of 1727.

As a romantic ruin, Furness Abbey has attracted and inspired antiquarian poets, painters and novelists since at least the 18th century. Today the red sandstone remains of the Cistercian abbey, standing in the secluded sheltered Vale of Nightshade, are no longer fringed with overgrowth, but they are no less inspiring. The valley's isolated setting, between Morecambe Bay and the hills of the Lake District, has made it all the more attractive to pursuers of the Picturesque.

William Gilpin included an illustration in his *Observations Relative Chiefly to Picturesque Beauty* (1786) where he described how the abbey 'has suffered, from the hands of time, only such depredations as picturesque beauty requires'. The novelist Mrs Radcliffe celebrated 'the character of the deserted ruin' in her *Journey Made in the Summer of 1794* (1795) savouring 'the luxurious melancholy which the view of it inspires'. William Wordsworth wrote an introduction to Joseph Wilkinson's *Select Views in Cumberland, Westmoreland and Lancashire* (1810), which included a print of the abbey church; however, the poet wrote to a friend that the 'etchings, or whatever they may be called, are … intolerable'. The separate publication of Wordsworth's introduction as his *Guide to the Lakes* (1835) made Furness even more popular.

Two drawings by Thomas Hearne, made in 1777, were engraved for Hearne and Byrne's *Antiquities of Great Britain*

Thomas Hearne (1774–1817), *The West Aspect of Furness Abbey, Cumberland, c* 1777, watercolour, pencil, pen and ink (Dove Cottage and the Wordsworth Museum, Grasmere)

(1786). In the accompanying text Hearne analyses the architectural styles, comparing Norman and Gothic features at Furness, with an artist's eye for detail. Traditionally the dating of ruins had been left to antiquarians expert in analysing documentation. Edward Dayes painted here in 1795, J M W Turner in 1797 and John Charles Buckler in 1814, among many others. A fine aquatint of the abbey church from the south-west by Theodore Fielding was published in Fielding and Walton's *Picturesque Tour of the English Lakes* (1821). Early photographers, including Roger Fenton and Francis Frith, came to record Furness from 1856.

Founded by the Savigniac order and taken over by the Cistercians around 1150, Furness became the second wealthiest Cistercian abbey in England (after Fountains) by the time of the Dissolution (1536–40), when it was the first of the major monasteries to be dissolved. The lead was stripped from the roofs in July 1537, even before the monks had left. It eventually became part of the estate of the Cavendish family of Holker Hall.

The Furness railway opened in 1847 with a station next to the abbey; soon after, in the 1850s, the Furness Abbey Hotel was built immediately adjacent. Wordsworth lamented in 1845: 'Many of the trees which embowered the ruin have been felled to make way for this pestilential nuisance.' John Ruskin later mourned the ruined abbeys of England, noting that they were being 'shaken down, as my own sweet Furness is fast being, by the luggage trains'. With the expansion of the hotel and station to meet the demands of day-trippers from northern industrial towns Furness was able to offer conference facilities. For example, around 1910 hundreds of delegates from the United Association of Bakers and Confectioners filled the abbey for their commemorative group photograph. The hotel was demolished in 1953.

Thomas Smith of Derby (fl 1747–67), *A Church Procession Entering Furness Abbey, c* 1750, oil on canvas (Private Collection)

Goodrich Castle, Herefordshire

GUARDING ENGLAND'S BORDER WITH WALES, Goodrich Castle is first recorded around 1101–2. This fortified baronial palace of the Talbot family (created Earls of Shrewsbury in the 15th century) has been uninhabited since the late 16th century, though it was briefly occupied by both Parliamentary and Royalist forces during the Civil War.

Ferry boats laden with pilgrims of the Picturesque glide along the River Wye in Thomas Hearne's fine prospect of Goodrich Castle, standing on the crest of the steep hillside. The castle looks down on the wooded valley of Symonds Yat, about three miles south of Ross-on-Wye, and is one of the early highlights of a classic excursion, the Wye Valley tour. The river flows south to Tintern Abbey and then joins the River Severn below Chepstow, affording countless picturesque prospects reflected in the clear waters along its serpentine path. Over two days and from the comfort of pleasure boats, admirers could enjoy an almost endlessly varied succession of romantic pictorial compositions in nature, unfolding along the slow, looping river like scenery in a theatre.

The popular theorist of the Picturesque, William Gilpin, took such a tour in the summer of 1770 and his *Observations on the River Wye* (1782) is the most influential of all guides to picturesque travel. He describes the prospect of the ruins of Goodrich Castle, just as Hearne paints it:

> … we rested on our oars to examine it. A reach of the river, forming a noble bay, is spread before the eye. The bank, on the right, is steep, and covered with wood; beyond which a bold promontory shoots out, crowned with a castle, rising among the trees.

Gilpin told a friend: 'If you have never navigated the Wye you have seen nothing … the whole is such a display of picturesque scenery that it is beyond any commendation.' By the end of the 18th century Gilpin's *Observations* had run into five editions and at least eight commercial pleasure boats were operating between Ross and Chepstow every summer. William Wordsworth must have had a copy of Gilpin's book when he visited the Wye valley in 1798 and wrote his poem *Lines Written a Few Miles above Tintern Abbey*.

Thomas Hearne (1744–1817), *Goodrich Castle on the Wye, c* 1790, watercolour, pen and ink, chalk and pencil (Yale Center for British Art, Paul Mellon Collection, USA)

Hadleigh Castle, Essex

JOHN CONSTABLE'S *HADLEIGH CASTLE* is one of the classic images of English Romanticism. In contrast to his masterpieces evoking Suffolk's rural calm such as *The Hay-Wain* (1821, National Gallery, London), here he chose to paint the ruins of a 13th-century castle on the north shore of the Thames estuary as the clouds clear after a stormy night. There can be little doubt that the subject was autobiographical, for his wife Maria died of consumption in November 1828 and the following month he told his brother: 'The face of the World is totally changed to me.'

Constable probably began this painting in 1828 or early 1829, using a sketch made some 15 years before. For all its emotional impact, rooted in personal grief, the painting follows the artistic and literary convention of using ruins to convey melancholy and stir a sense of the Sublime in the viewer. Reflection on the brevity of human life had become a fashionable response to such scenes of devastation before the grandeur of nature.

When Constable first visited Hadleigh in 1814 he wrote to his fiancée Maria Bicknell: 'At Hadleigh there is a ruin of a castle which from its situation is really a fine place – it commands a view of the Kent hills the Nore and the North Foreland & looking many miles to sea.' We may assume he brought Maria here to see the ruins and the view. By contrast, when he exhibited this painting at the Royal Academy in 1829 he accompanied it with the following lines from James Thomson's *Summer*:

The desert joys
Wildly, through all his melancholy bounds
Rude ruins glitter; and the briny deep,
Seen from some pointed promontory's top,
Far to the dim horizon's utmost verge
Restless, reflects a floating gleam.

Hubert de Burgh, Chief Justiciar to Henry III, built Hadleigh Castle in 1230 on the edge of flatlands, overlooking the Essex marshes. Nine years later, the young King Henry confiscated it while still unfinished. Henry III continued construction on the castle, but most of the remains seen today date from the 14th century when Edward III took possession and refortified the castle. Edward III's work on the castle included strengthening its defences and making it a more fitting royal residence. The eastern towers date from this period of refortification in the 1360s. Gradually royal interest in Hadleigh waned and its royal associations finally ended in 1552 when it was sold to Lord Riche by Edward VI. Lord Riche seems to have used the castle as a source of building stone and it had become a ruin by the 17th century. There is some evidence that the south-east tower acted as an observation point for revenue officers during the 18th and 19th centuries.

John Constable (1776–1837), *Hadleigh Castle, The Mouth of the Thames. Morning after a Stormy Night*, 1829, oil on canvas (Yale Center for British Art, Paul Mellon Collection, USA)

Hadrian's Wall, Northumberland and Cumbria

O N THE TOP OF HADRIAN'S WALL a Roman centurion scowls at a family of British workers in William Bell Scott's imaginative painting. He finds the idle natives playing dice while waiting for their pot to boil. Beyond, others labour to build the Wall while deflecting arrows fired by their northern attackers. The finished stretch of the Wall snakes along the cliff top into the distance: the landscape is painted with a love of dense clear detail that Bell Scott learnt from the Pre-Raphaelites. He painted this mural for Walter and Pauline Trevelyan of Wallington Hall in Northumberland while teaching at the School of Design in Newcastle. He clearly took great pains in researching Roman dress. Even the Wall had to be accurate, as he had a section sent to his studio to copy.

Fred Taylor's advertising poster for the London & North Eastern Railway is a brilliant example of how an artist can match his design to his medium as he uses the bold blocks of printed colour to achieve maximum visual impact. Taylor specialised in railway posters of historic sites in the 'golden age' of poster production, before the creation of British Rail in 1947 ended the need for competitive advertising between the companies.

The Roman Emperor Hadrian ordered the construction of a great wall in the years AD 122–8. Hadrian's Wall, the largest of all Roman frontier constructions, ran for 73 miles, from Wallsend-on-Tyne to Bowness on the Solway Firth. The troops on the Wall included infantry and cavalry drawn from all corners of the Roman Empire. The Wall was finally abandoned as a frontier in the late 4th to early 5th century AD. Today this World Heritage Site remains the chief monument of Roman Britain.

The forts at Chesters, Housesteads, Vindolanda and Corbridge are the most excavated ones on the Wall today (and are open to visitors). Antiquarian descriptions of the Wall date from the 16th century, with the first important survey made by William Camden, author of *Britannia* (1586), a description of England, Scotland and Wales. The Wall suffered after the Jacobite Rebellion of 1745, for stones were taken to build a new road linking Carlisle to Newcastle. Further quarrying for building stone followed the agricultural boom in the border uplands.

One of the Wall's protectors and excavators was John Clayton, who inherited the Chesters estate from 1832 and bought up further land along the Wall until his death in 1890. He acquired five of the major Roman sites, owned a large part of the central section of the Wall and founded a museum of his finds at Chesters. The present museum building dates from 1890; finds from the sites are displayed in Clayton's black-japanned showcases.

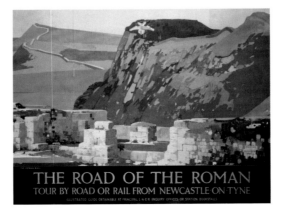

Fred Taylor (1875–1963), *The Roman Wall.*
The Road of the Roman, 1932, poster
(National Railway Museum)

William Bell Scott
(1811–90), *The
Building of the Roman
Wall*, 1857, mural
painting (National
Trust, Wallington Hall)

63

Hailes Abbey, Gloucestershire

IN OCTOBER 1242, stranded at sea and fearing for his life, Richard, Earl of Cornwall, King of the Romans, vowed to found a religious house, should he survive. Three years later his brother, King Henry III, granted him the Manor of Hailes to do so. The Cistercian order began building their abbey church near the foot of the Cotswolds in 1246. Richard's son, Edmund, presented the abbey with a phial – said to contain the blood of Christ – which he had purchased in 1267 from the Count of Flanders. It carried a guarantee of authenticity from the Patriach of Jerusalem, who later became Pope Urban IV. A shrine (measuring some 3 × 2½ metres) was built for the holy relic behind the high altar and the east end was extended to provide a processional aisle and ring of chapels. Hailes was now guaranteed a steady stream of pilgrims and became one of England's great centres of pilgrimage. For example, in 1533 the vicar of Kineton wrote 'you would wonder how they come by flocks out of the West Country to many images but chiefly to the Blood of Hailes'. On 28 October 1538 the holy blood was taken to London by the commissioners responsible for the Dissolution of the monasteries. On 24 November the Bishop of Rochester displayed the phial while preaching and declared it to be 'honey clarified and coloured with saffron, as had been evidently proved before the King and Council'.

The abbey was sold by the Crown to Richard Andrews, a dealer in monastic property, in 1542 and the church was probably demolished soon after. At the beginning of the 17th century it was sold to Sir John Tracy. His family used the abbot's house and west range of the cloister as their secondary residence until the 1730s. The house and formal flat gardens are recorded in Johannes Kip's bird's-eye view, one of 65 plates he drew and engraved to illustrate *The Ancient and Present State of Gloucestershire* (1712) by Robert Atkyns. Despite the engraved inscription, 'Hales Abbey the Seat of the Lord Tracy' shows no evidence of any ruins. By contrast, they are the main feature, set in rolling hills, in a detailed watercolour from around 1748 by Thomas Robins the Elder. The topographical artist is now best known for his series of paintings of the rococo gardens at Painswick. By the late 18th century buildings had been demolished and the site was used as a farmyard.

Hailes became an attraction again following excavations by the Bristol and Gloucestershire Archaeological Society in 1899, when a museum was founded at the site; the first guidebook for the site was published in 1928. Hailes became even more accessible when the Great Western Railway gave the site its own station, Hailes Halt.

Thomas Robins the Elder (1716–70), *Hailes Abbey, c* 1748, watercolour (National Trust, on loan to Cheltenham Museum and Art Gallery)

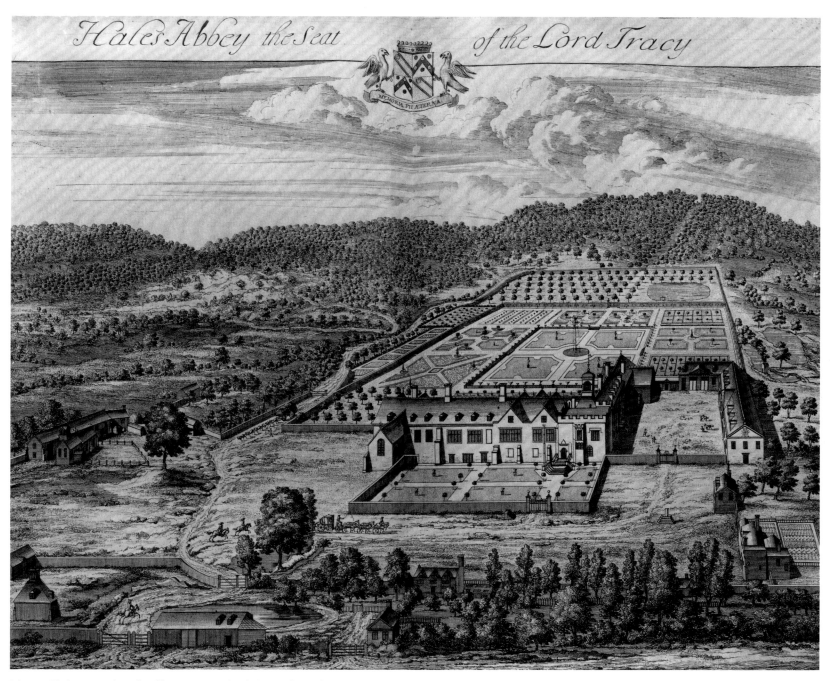

Johannes Kip (1653–1722), *Hailes Abbey*, 1712, engraving (Private Collection)

Helmsley Castle, North Yorkshire

IN THOMAS GIRTIN'S VIEW OF HELMSLEY CASTLE a solitary poacher or gamekeeper steps through the fresh snow to take a pot shot, probably at a passing rabbit. The blinding effect of bright sun and blue skies on snow is brilliantly conveyed, with the ruins defined by just a few hints of stonework and shadows. Like the same artist's seemingly simple view of Dunstanburgh (*see* p 48), the small watercolour puts the viewer right in the scene by keeping conventions of pictorial composition, of foreground and middle ground, to a minimum.

The imaginative reconstruction by F W Hulme of domestic life in 'Helmsley Hall' before the Civil War is typical of the nostalgic images of England in the 'Olden Time' published for Victorian day-trippers. Coats of arms in the windows and plasterwork allude to the ancient lineage of the de Roos family, as does a helmet, while a mounted trophy head and horns hints at the deer park outside. Such fantasies were published in series and later issued in volumes, the most successful of which were Joseph Nash's *Mansions of England in the Olden Time* (1839–49) and Samuel Carter Hall's *Baronial Halls, Picturesque Edifices, and Ancient Churches of England* (1844–7). While Europe was in revolution, such popular images of the English aristocracy at home portrayed them as benign guardians of the nation's heritage.

The market town of Helmsley in North Yorkshire was already thriving at a crossroads near the River Rye before Walter Espec established his castle there by the 1120s. He had amassed land under King Henry I as Justiciar of the Forests and Justiciar of the Northern Counties and carefully sited his castle at the centre of his estates. A patron of scholars, he also founded Kirkham Priory in 1122 and in 1131 granted land to establish Rievaulx Abbey. After his death in 1154 his estates passed to his sister's husband, Peter de Roos, in whose family they remained until the 17th century. By the mid-13th century two walled parks were created adjacent to the castle for recreational hunting of deer by the lord and his guests. A circuitous approach to the castle, around the outer earthworks, was also made at that time to impress visitors.

Sir George Manners, nephew of Edmund de Roos, inherited Helmsley Castle in 1508.

At the Dissolution of the monasteries, his son supported the removal of Abbot Edward of Rievaulx and purchased the abbey site and estates. The castle's life as a ruin began in the Civil War after Royalist troops surrendered to the Parliamentarian army there in 1644; the commander in charge of the siege was ordered to 'slight' the castle in order to render it defenceless. In the 18th century a new mansion, Duncombe Park, was built by a London banker, set within the former parks of the castle and the lands of Rievaulx Abbey. The ruins survived as romantic features to prompt reflection by guests strolling along Rievaulx Terrace and the northern Yew Walk in the parkland (*see* p 106). Charles Duncombe was created Lord Feversham in 1826 and Duncombe Park remains the residence of his descendants.

After F W Hulme (1816–84), *Helmsley Hall, Yorkshire, c* 1845, lithograph (Private Collection)

Thomas Girtin (1775–1802), *Helmsley Castle, The East Tower*, *c* 1796, watercolour (Private Collection)

Ironbridge, Shropshire

AT COALBROOKDALE IN THE SEVERN GORGE IN SHROPSHIRE the world's first iron bridge crosses the River Severn. Designed by Thomas Farnolls Pritchard and constructed between 1777 and 1781, it soon became a symbol of the promise of the Industrial Revolution and gave its name to the town that grew up around it.

Funding for the bridge came from Abraham Darby, whose grandfather had introduced the use of coke to smelt iron, and the bridge was built with iron from the Coalbrookdale foundry. This pioneering use of iron in architecture had many heirs, most notably the great railway stations of the 19th century such as Paddington and St Pancras in London.

Darby commissioned the painter Michael Angelo Rooker to commemorate the new bridge in a view that would put Coalbrookdale on the international map. In 1786 Thomas Jefferson purchased a print after Rooker's view and later hung it in his official residence in Washington when he was President of the United States. Rooker had trained under Paul Sandby and became principal scene painter at the Theatre Royal, Haymarket in London. As in his view of Buildwas Abbey (*see* p 31), he animates the topographical record with local characters. In William Williams's view an enthusiastic sightseer stands up in a ferry boat to point out the bridge while his lady companion reaches out to steady him, with the smoking chimneystacks of Coalbrookdale in the distance.

Coalbrookdale was already on the tourist itinerary as industrial sites were added to the list of essential places to see for those in search of the Sublime. Arthur Young, in his *Annals of Agriculture and Other Useful Arts* (1784–1809) found Coalbrookdale 'a very romantic spot … the noise of the gorges, mills, &c. with all their vast machinery, the flames bursting from the furnaces with the burning of the coal and the smoak of the lime kilns, are altogether sublime'.

The cast-iron structure with its romantic setting still inspires artists in its own right. Like his brother Paul, John Nash sought structure in landscape and here contrasts the sharp, web-like skeletal frame of the bridge with the hillside of houses.

William Williams (1740–1800), *The Iron Bridge*, 1780, oil on canvas (Ironbridge Gorge Museum, Telford)

John Nash (1893–1977), *Ironbridge, Shropshire*, c 1960, watercolour (Private Collection)

Michael Angelo Rooker (1746–1801), *The Cast Iron Bridge near Coalbrookdale*, 1780, watercolour (Aberdeen Art Gallery & Museums)

Kenilworth Castle, Warwickshire

THE RUINS OF KENILWORTH CASTLE are more firmly rooted in the English countryside than are the gnarled old oaks and birch being felled in the foreground of James Ward's prospect. His painting is an English reply to the celebrated masterpiece by Peter Paul Rubens, *A View of the Château de Steen* (National Gallery, London), which Ward had first seen in 1803. The painting also inspired some of John Constable's best-known works. At the time Ward was painting, in 1840, Kenilworth was one of the most popular ruins in England. Between 1825 and 1849 visitors to the Royal Academy's annual exhibition would have found more views of Kenilworth than of any other named place in Britain.

For the visit of Queen Elizabeth I in July 1575 Robert Dudley, Earl of Leicester, restored and enlarged Kenilworth Castle, regardless of expense. For 19 days she enjoyed the 'princely pleasures' of hunting, jousting, pageantry, music-making and the new Pleasure Garden. Water pageants and fireworks filled the vast lake, known as the Great Mere, outside the castle. The entertainment cost Dudley £1,000 per day. Host and guests expected the announcement of the queen's engagement to her favourite, but it never came.

In improving Kenilworth, Dudley was following a royal tradition. The castle had been founded around 1122 by Geoffrey de Clinton, chamberlain to Henry I, but within 50 years it was acquired by Henry II. King John extended the Norman castle in the 13th century and shortly before 1400 John of Gaunt built a hall and improved the private apartments to create a palace. King Henry V built a banqueting house and Henry VIII enlarged the lodgings. The castle was 'slighted' after falling into Parliamentary hands in the Civil War. The officer in charge of the demolition did as little damage as possible, bought the

castle and moved into Leicester's great gatehouse. Left unoccupied after the Restoration in 1660, the castle deteriorated into a ruin.

Visitor interest in Kenilworth prompted a detailed pair of prospects, complete with numbered keys identifying each building, by William Dugdale and Wenceslaus Hollar, published in 1656. With the publication of Sir Walter Scott's best-selling historical novel *Kenilworth* in 1821, the visit of Elizabeth I entered the popular imagination. The subject of the novel, set against the spectacle of the royal entertainments, is the mysterious death of Dudley's wife whose presence is kept secret from the queen. J M W Turner painted a view of Kenilworth showing Dudley receiving Elizabeth I (currently untraced) probably as an illustration to Scott's novel; his other view painted around 1830 can be seen in the Fine Arts Museum of San Francisco, USA.

The Hudson River school painter Thomas Cole made studies of Kenilworth in 1841 at the start of his European tour when he visited his relatives (the American painter was born

Thomas Cole (1801–48), *The Ruins of Kenilworth Castle*, 1841, oil on board
(Juniata College Museum of Art, Huntingdon, Pennsylvania, USA)

in Bolton-le-Moor, Lancashire). Shortly before setting out from America he wrote 'although American scenery was often so fine, we feel the want of associations such as cling to scenes in the old world'. An admirer of Constable and Turner, Cole painted in the open air, making the most of recent commercial developments of artists' millboard and prepared oil paint in collapsible tubes. Cole wrote home to his wife: 'the ivy-clad towers, roofless halls, whose floors are covered with green turf and flowers, and cropped by flocks of sheep … inspired me with a melancholy pleasure'. However, by the time Henry James visited, as he wrote in 1877, Kenilworth was so popular that he had to get through 'a row of ancient peddlers outside the castle wall, hawking twopenny pamphlets and photographs'.

James Ward (1769–1859), *Kenilworth Castle, Warwickshire*, 1840, oil on panel (Yale Center for British Art, Paul Mellon Collection, USA)

Kenwood, The Iveagh Bequest, London

WILLIAM MURRAY, LORD CHIEF JUSTICE, 1st Earl of Mansfield, purchased Kenwood in 1755 and it soon became celebrated as the home of the great judge. Jeremy Bentham recalled coming to Kenwood uninvited, as a law student, 'as a lover to the shrine of his mistress, in the hope that chance might throw him his way'. This 'celebrity home' became the subject of cheap engravings, produced to illustrate travel guides, after Murray employed the architect Robert Adam to extend and remodel it from 1764–79. Adam published his own set of engravings to record the commission and to capitalise on the prominence of the villa in order to attract more patrons.

Kenwood's prominence as one of the landmarks of outer London is clear from T Ramsey's view of 1755 from the pond above Hampstead, which shows Kenwood in the distance. The suburban villa, standing midway between the fashionable villages of Hampstead and Highgate, was on a popular riding route from central London. It afforded fine prospects across London and its skyline, as far as Greenwich and the Kent hills beyond.

In 1793 David Murray, 2nd Earl of Mansfield, commissioned the landscape architect Humphry Repton to produce a 'Red Book' of designs for the landscape gardens around Kenwood. Repton painted watercolour views of the house and gardens as he found them and then painted separate details of his proposed improvements; these details were bound in as overlays to the main views so that his client could see his garden as if 'before and after' Repton's remodelling. The view illustrated here is from the south, as Repton and passers-by would have found Kenwood, looking from the adjacent estate over a public path.

The villa soon became renowned for its garden setting. According to J C Loudon in his book *The Suburban Gardener and Villa Companion* (1838), Kenwood 'is, beyond all question, the finest country residence in the suburbs of London … It is, indeed, difficult to imagine a more retired or more romantic spot, and yet of such extent, so near a great metropolis.'

Kenwood opened to the public in 1928 as The Iveagh Bequest, home of the greatest private collection of old master paintings given to the British nation in the 20th century. The gift of Edward Cecil Guinness, 1st Earl of Iveagh, includes masterpieces by Rembrandt, Vermeer, Van Dyck, Gainsborough, Reynolds and Turner. Londoners and their guests come to see the paintings, prospects, gardens, concerts and the changing seasons. Kenwood has also found a wider international audience as a setting in the film *Notting Hill* (1999).

Giovanni Vitalba (1738–92) and Benedetto Pastorini (c 1746–1803), *View of the South Front of the Villa at Kenwood*, 1774, engraving for Robert Adam's *Works in Architecture* (1774) (English Heritage, Kenwood)

T Ramsey (fl 1755), *Heath House, Hampstead*, 1755, oil on canvas (Private Collection). Kenwood can be seen in the distance.

Humphry Repton (1752–1818), *Kenwood, the South Front, c* 1793, watercolour (The Earl of Mansfield, Scone Palace)

Kirby Hall, Northamptonshire

SAMUEL EDMUND WALLER'S PAINTING *IN CHANCERY* captures the thrill of visiting an abandoned country house as passing riders tread gingerly across the threshold of Kirby Hall. John Piper's stark moonlit scene goes one step further in his more universal image of ruins, presenting Kirby as the architectural equivalent of a *memento mori*, a reminder of death.

Kirby Hall was completed by one of Queen Elizabeth I's favourite courtiers, Sir Christopher Hatton, Lord Chancellor, in the hope of entertaining her on her annual 'progresses' around England. She never came, he died in debt in 1591 and a contemporary described him as a 'mere vegetable of the court that sprung up at night and sank again at his noon'. However, his nephew and heir, also Christopher Hatton, did receive King James I at Kirby in 1612 and 1619, and his queen, Anne of Denmark, in 1605.

The Thorpe family of masons probably built Kirby Hall, drawing upon Sebastiano Serlio's *L'Architettura* (1537–51) and on French pattern books for the wealth of fashionable carved decoration. The north front was remodelled between 1638 and 1640 by Nicholas Stone who had worked as Master-Mason under the court architect Inigo Jones on the Whitehall Banqueting House for James I (completed in 1622). For many years scholars believed that Kirby was the work of Inigo Jones himself.

In 1694 Kirby Hall was known for having 'ye finest garden in England'. George London had visited in 1693 and probably advised on the design of an elaborate parterre in the Dutch court taste of William III and Mary II. The garden was enriched with trees and shrubs in tubs, along with statues of classical gods and urns. Its fame was more probably due to the rare plants it could boast, such as 'narcissus of Japan', 'hyacinth of Peru' and 'ye soape tree from China'.

Kirby declined from the early 18th century, with sales of its contents in 1772 and 1824. Four years later the historian John Nichols noted that it was 'now dismantled and going fast to decay'. The house did not fall prey to the usual agents of decline, such as fire, quarrying of the house for building materials or vandalism; rather it gradually became a deserted shell, which attracted visitors curious to see its melancholy state. The Revd Canon

James vividly described 'the very action of decomposition going on, the crumbling stucco of the ceiling feeding the vampire ivy, the tattered tapestry yet hanging on the wall, the picture flapping in its broken frame'. In 1844 Samuel Carter Hall (*The Baronial Halls, Picturesque Edifices, and Ancient Churches of England*, 1844–7) found how 'farm-servants sleep surrounded by exquisite carvings; one room … decorated with a fine old fire-place … served, at the time of the artist's visit, the purpose of a dog-kennel'. Kirby had become the English equivalent of the picturesque Roman ruins inhabited by Arcadian peasants in Nicholas Poussin's 17th-century masterpieces of classical landscape painting.

However, picturesque decay did not appeal to some artists, for Kirby seems intact in the architectural perspective by Thomas Allom. A Victorian architect who made topographical drawings, mostly of buildings, for publication in books, Allom produced views of Norham Castle and Osborne House (*see* pp 88 and 96) that are similarly measured and precise.

John Piper (1903–92), *Kirby Hall, Northamptonshire*, 1944, autolithograph (Private Collection)

Samuel Edmund Waller
(1850–1903), *In Chancery*, 1884,
oil on canvas (English Heritage)

Thomas Allom (1804–72), *Kirby Hall*, *c* 1850, pencil, pen and wash (English Heritage)

Kirkham Priory, North Yorkshire

A S IN HIS VIEWS OF BUILDWAS AND BYLAND ABBEYS (*see* pp 30 and 33), John Sell Cotman sees the north gatehouse of Kirkham Priory with a fresh eye for structure expressed through extreme crisp tonal contrasts. The details of sculptural embellishment in the initial pencil drawing do not tempt his brush as, with the drawing master's methodical approach, he lays clear washes to define sunshine soaking into masonry. Amidst dishevelled fencing and uneven terrain the crumbling ruin is in the most picturesque condition, as it seems to sink back into nature. No greater contrast can be imagined than with the earlier view by Samuel Buck, where the topographer's ambition to record the whole forlorn site lacks Cotman's eye for the essentials.

The Augustinian community of canons at Kirkham Priory was founded between 1122 and 1130 by Walter Espec, Lord of Helmsley, who later founded Rievaulx Abbey for monks of the Cistercian order. The north gatehouse was built in the 13th century by the de Roos lords of Helmsley and is enriched with their family heraldry and with figurative sculpture. Cotman's watercolour records a carving of the Crucifixion immediately above the arch of the gateway; it had gone by 1843 when the artist William Richardson painted a similar view. Fortunately the sculptures of St George and the Dragon (on the left side in the painting) and David and Goliath (on the right) still remain in position. Above each group in Cotman's painting, as today, shields display the arms of the Scrope, de Roos and de Fortibus families. Above is a seated figure of Christ flanked by St Philip and St Bartholomew, with shields with the arms of de Clare, England, de Roos and Vaux. They proclaimed the status of the founders of the priory, which became a favourite burial place of the Lords of Helmsley between 1258 and 1343.

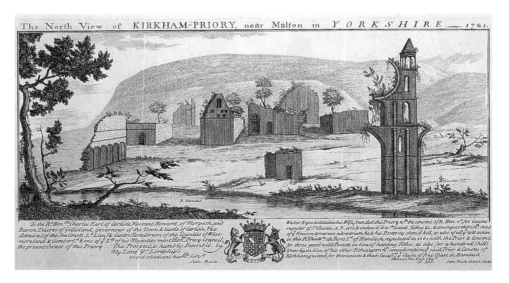

Samuel Buck (1696–1779), *The North View of Kirkham Priory*, 1721, engraving (English Heritage)

John Sell Cotman (1782–1842), *Kirkham Abbey*, 1805, watercolour (York Art Gallery)

Landguard Fort, Suffolk

LANDGUARD FORT GUARDS THE SUFFOLK COAST just south of Felixstowe. Henry VIII fortified this site in the Orwell estuary in the 1540s and it remained in military use, near the docks at Felixstowe, until soon after the Second World War. After the polygonal fort with angle bastions had been developed in brick in the 18th century it was enlarged in the Napoleonic Wars. The present entrance and parade ground date from 1875. Today the fort stands adjacent to the Languard container terminal, which caters for the largest ships in the world. However, the shingle spit between the sea and the fort provides a nature reserve for migrating birds.

Thomas Gainsborough moved to Ipswich in 1752 and was commissioned to paint a view by Philip Thicknesse, who was appointed Lieutenant Governor of the fort in 1753. Thicknesse requested 'the particulars of the Fort, the adjacent hills, and the distant view of Harwich, in order to form a landscape of the Yachts passing the garrison under the salute of the guns, of the size of a pannel [sic] over my chimney piece'. Gainsborough was just establishing himself as a portrait painter in the prosperous market town and port when Thicknesse first visited his studio. There he noted portraits 'stiffly painted … but when I turned my eyes to the little landscapes and drawings, I was charmed'. For his portrait (one in the St Louis Art Museum, USA is traditionally identified as of him) Thicknesse went to Francis Hayman, but he struck the same pose, lounging against a tree, as Gainsborough used for his foreground figure in the Landguard view. Gainsborough's career only really took off when he combined his love of landscape with portraiture by placing his sitters in outdoor settings, a formula with which he flourished after he moved to Bath in 1759. Thicknesse became friends with Gainsborough and he praised the artist's work in magazine reviews; his biography of Gainsborough was published in 1788.

Thicknesse recalled that Gainsborough's painting of the prospect was destroyed. This earlier painting has only recently been rediscovered (by Anthony Mould) and is published here for the first time. Gainsborough's view of Landguard was long known, as was the fort itself, from an engraving by Thomas Major, published in 1754, and from the claim made by Thicknesse that his commission, both for the painting and engraving, helped to launch the artist's successful career. The view illustrated here is painted from a slightly different angle from the version that Major engraved. It is a rare example of Gainsborough painting a topographical view. In the 1760s he warned a potential patron 'the Subject altogether, as well as figures etc must be of his own Brain'.

Architectural evidence supports the dating of Gainsborough's view to the 1750s, for Landguard Fort was rebuilt between 1744 and 1751; however, it is possible on stylistic grounds that this painting might be as early as c 1743–4, showing a speculative view. The painting shows two of the five bastions (Chapel Bastion on the left; Holland's Bastion on the right) with the gatehouse and chapel between them. This central building has been enlarged by the artist who must have been confused for he combined the gatehouse with the chapel and guardhouse. The latter did not extend back into the fort's parade ground as he paints it. These errors may have prompted the painting of a second version (the one that was engraved) and, indeed, Gainsborough's reluctance to tackle topography again. He also shows to the right of the guardhouse the Lieutenant Governor's House and Officers' Quarters, built of brick. The Soldiers' Barracks stand behind the guardhouse. Outside the fort he records parts of the former Governor's House.

Detail of the view of the fort

Attributed to Thomas Gainsborough (1727–88), *A View of Harwich from the Cliffs above Landguard Fort*, *c* 1743–53, oil on canvas (Private Collection)

Launceston Castle, Cornwall

THE CASTLE ON THE EASTERN BORDER OF CORNWALL AT LAUNCESTON was originally built in timber by Robert de Mortain, half-brother of William the Conqueror, soon after the Norman Conquest. With the construction of the assize courts and jail on this site, Launceston remained an administrative centre until 1840. The last hanging took place in the courtyard in 1821, the jail was demolished in 1842 and the castle then became a public park and garden. It still dominates the main route into Cornwall today.

This fine prospect of the 13th-century castle by Hendrik Frans de Cort is rich in topographical detail. The view is taken from St Catherine's Hill and has been extended to include the main points of historic interest. The condition of the north gate (to the left) suggests that the view dates from before 1764, for in that year the gate was partially demolished and was subsequently pillaged for building materials. The painting also records the motte and bailey before they were landscaped in the late 18th century. As de Cort only became a Master in his native Antwerp in 1770, and is not known to have settled in England until 1790, the view may be based on earlier images. Another later loss is the defended bridge over the moat, two-thirds of which was destroyed in 1834, along with the moat, when St Thomas Road was constructed. Left of the castle can be seen Newport, the Church of St Thomas and the remains of St Stephen's Priory. To the right of the castle gate stands the watch or 'witches' tower, which fell in 1830, with the centre of Launceston itself further to the right.

Painting on a smooth panel in the Netherlandish tradition, de Cort has met his English client's need for topographical information while creating a composition that could hang among works by the 17th-century masters in a country house collection. By contrast, J M W Turner chose a more dramatic distant view for his watercolour. The rider in the foreground may be an allusion to George Fox, founder of the Society of Friends, who was imprisoned at Launceston for refusing to remove his hat before a magistrate after his arrest in 1656.

J M W Turner (1775–1851), *Launceston, Cornwall*, 1827, watercolour (Private Collection)

Hendrik Frans de Cort (1742–1810), *Launceston Castle, Cornwall*, c 1790, oil on panel (English Heritage, Launceston Castle)

Lindisfarne Priory, Northumberland

LINDISFARNE PRIORY STANDS ON HOLY ISLAND, two miles off the coast of Northumberland to which it is linked by a tidal causeway. In this coastal view by the Scottish painter Edmund Thornton Crawford the artist is attracted as much by the bony remains of the priory as by its island setting, and the fine prospect across the water to Lindisfarne Castle. With the golden sunlight, grazing cattle and sheep, Crawford's composition draws upon the Dutch 17th-century masters such as Aelbert Cuyp and Meindert Hobbema, with echoes of the Van de Veldes in the boats sitting in glassy shallows. Thomas Girtin, by contrast, takes us right to the foot of the ruins, filling his sheet of paper so that they seem to tower over us, as in his dramatic views of Dunstanburgh and Helmsley (*see* pp 48 and 67). While meeting the fashionable taste for the Sublime he has set himself the artistic challenge of painting tonal variations within silhouettes and shadows.

St Aidan, first bishop of the northern Northumbrians, founded the monastery in AD 635. It became an important centre of Christianity in England and a place of pilgrimage after the enshrinement of St Cuthbert's body in AD 698 when, 11 years after his death, his body was found to be miraculously preserved. The monks at Lindisfarne wrote and illuminated the celebrated Lindisfarne Gospels (British Library) either for the enshrinement or soon after. Miracles at St Cuthbert's shrine made Lindisfarne the major pilgrimage centre of Northumbria and the wealthy beneficiary of royal gifts. However, as visitor numbers grew, disrupting religious life, Lindisfarne also attracted criminals and political pretenders seeking refuge.

Frequent Viking raids from the late 8th century led to the abandonment of the priory a century later. The island was finally resettled by the monks of Durham in the 12th century, when the present priory, of which only extensive ruins remain, was built. Cuthbert's body was removed to Durham Cathedral. Henry VIII's commissioners closed the priory in 1537. Temporary timber defences were erected in the harbour area in 1542–5 and between 1565 and 1571 the castle was reconstructed in stone.

Around 1613 lead was stripped from the roofs of the priory, but much of the church survived into the 18th century. Its gradual decline into a romantic ruin can be traced through views painted by artists, such as Girtin and Crawford. From 1902 the castle was rebuilt for the proprietor of *Country Life* magazine by Sir Edwin Lutyens, with a walled garden by Gertrude Jeckyll. Holy Island is still a place of Christian pilgrimage today.

Thomas Girtin (1775–1802), *Lindisfarne Priory, c* 1797, pencil and watercolour (Fitzwilliam Museum, University of Cambridge)

Edmund Thornton Crawford (1806–85), *Lindisfarne Priory, Holy Island*, 1851, oil on canvas (Private Collection)

Marble Hill, London

WHEN RICHARD WILSON'S VIEW OF MARBLE HILL was exhibited at the Society of Artists in 1762, simply entitled *View on the Thames near Twickenham*, Horace Walpole recognised the home of his elderly neighbour, Mrs Howard, and noted it in his catalogue. This became one of Wilson's most popular British landscape paintings, prompting him to paint at least four versions. The choice of an oblique viewpoint, from the footpath in front of Ham House, enabled Wilson to screen out the adjacent houses that Augustin Heckell shows in his more topographical record. The idyllic setting is much the same today, but for the embankment of the river and the greater volume of boats. Wilson's elegant trees, poised in the raking sun, may be his touch of artistic licence.

The heart of the celebrated prospect from Richmond Hill, Marble Hill is the best preserved of the 18th-century villas and gardens that made up the 'English Arcadia' along the Thames at Richmond and Twickenham. The estate was purchased, and the perfect Palladian villa built, for Henrietta Howard, later Countess of Suffolk, the mistress of King George II. Described by her great admirer and neighbour Alexander Pope, as 'a woman of reason', Mrs Howard attracted the finest designers and craftspeople of her era to create Marble Hill between 1724 and 1729. With her retirement from court to Marble Hill in 1734 Pope felt crowded out by her friends, lamenting 'there is a greater court now at Marble Hill than in Kensington, and God knows where it will end'.

The engraving of Marble Hill, published in 1749 after a topographical view by Heckell, illustrates how prominent the house would have been to passers-by and to the river traffic he records. Heckell's engraving was intended

James Mason (*c* 1710–85) after Augustin Heckell (*c* 1690–1770), *The Countess of Suffolk's House near Twickenham*, 1749, engraving (English Heritage, Marble Hill)

(according to the publisher's advertisements) for colouring and viewing 'in the Diagonal Mirrors'. It was reproduced and pirated for pocket books and periodicals such as the *Gentleman's Magazine*.

In her introduction to her pocket guide, *A Short Account of the Principal Seats in and about Twickenham* (1756), Henrietta Pye observed of Marble Hill and its neighbours 'that ladies in general, visit those places, as our young gentlemen do foreign parts, without answering any other end, than barely saying they have been there …These little excursions being commonly the only travel permitted to our sex & the only way we have of becoming at all acquainted with the Progress of Arts, I thought it might not be improper to throw together on paper, such remarks as occurred to me.' With the publication of Sir Walter Scott's *Heart of Midlothian* (1818) Marble Hill caught the interest of many more sightseers. As *The Builder* magazine noted in 1890 'thousands have scanned curiously from the deck of a river steamer' hoping to catch a glimpse of the avenue of elms where, in the historical novel, Jeanie Deans pleads with Queen Caroline for the life of her half-sister before Mrs Howard, as a lady-in-waiting, intervenes on her behalf. Unfortunately, the scene was really set in Richmond Park.

Unlike the 18th and 19th centuries, few of today's visitors to Marble Hill bring with them any familiarity with the writings of Walpole, Pope, Scott, Jonathan Swift and John Gay, for Mrs Howard's villa has rich literary associations. But it is appreciated no less as a complete Palladian villa, which was built only three miles from the more familiar example of this architectural genre, Lord Burlington's Chiswick House (*see* pp 40–1).

Richard Wilson (*c* 1713–82), *View on the Thames near Twickenham*, *c* 1762, oil on canvas (English Heritage, Marble Hill)

Middleham Castle, North Yorkshire

PAUL SANDBY SEES MIDDLEHAM CASTLE with the analytical eye of a former military surveyor and paints it with the disciplined brush of a drawing master to officers. A clump of trees and two knots of locals laden with purchases add picturesque interest, but essentially this is a crisp, factual account of ruined fortifications and their setting. The double dating by the artist (1762 and 1788) suggests he may have added the tree and figures at the later date, perhaps for engraving. A closer view of the castle, engraved after Sandby, was published in 1780. Thomas Girtin, by contrast, takes us in among the ruins so that we may savour all the mottled surfaces rising high above our heads.

The first castle at Middleham was an earthwork raised on a ridge after the Norman Conquest to control the upper reaches of Wensleydale. Richard, Duke of Gloucester, the future King Richard III, was granted the lordship of Middleham in 1472 by Edward IV. The 12th-century castle and estates had previously belonged to Richard, Earl of Warwick, who died at the Battle of Barnet in 1471. Richard married the Earl of Warwick's daughter in 1472. He had lived at Middleham as a young man between 1465 and 1468 when he had been trained in military and courtly skills. In 1478 he was granted the castles of Richmond and Helmsley, but Middleham remained his favourite. He also founded a college of priests at Middleham in 1478.

With the support of armed retainers from his northern estates Richard seized the throne and was crowned king in 1483. For much of his brief reign he lived in Westminster and in Nottingham Castle but he stayed at Middleham between 1 and 10 May 1484 during his royal progresses around England. King Richard III died at the Battle of Bosworth on 22 August 1485 after facing the army of Henry Tudor, who became King Henry VII after this victory. Henry VII then confiscated Middleham, but he never visited the castle. In 1604 King James I granted Middleham to Sir Henry Linley and in 1662 it was sold to Edward Wood, whose descendants owned it when Sandby and Girtin painted their views a century later. These watercolours are early records of the castle's decline into a ruinous state.

Thomas Girtin (1775–1802), *The Ruins of Middleham Castle, Yorkshire, c* 1797, pencil and watercolour on paper (Tate Collections)

Paul Sandby (1730/1–1809), *Middleham Castle, Yorkshire*, 1762 and 1788, watercolour (Private Collection)

Norham Castle, Northumberland

NORHAM CASTLE is one of the classic subjects of J M W Turner's art. As a motif to which he returned throughout his career, Norham has become associated with Turner almost as much as the façade of Rouen Cathedral is with Claude Monet and Mont Saint-Victoire is with Paul Cezanne. On this occasion, in 1824, Turner captures the moment of radiance on a late summer's evening when the setting sun slips behind the castle, transforming it into an ethereal deep purple silhouette. No longer dazzled by direct sunlight, we can see the tranquil scene below mirrored in the sparkling glassy waters. By comparison with Thomas Allom's more topographically informative treatment of the same scene, Turner is preoccupied with transient atmospheric effects, half a century before the French Impressionists.

Turner dated his success from his first painting of Norham Castle. He first visited the Tweed valley in 1797 and the following year he exhibited *Norham Castle, on the Tweed-summer's Morn* at the Royal Academy. One of his favourite subjects, Turner painted Norham Castle many times over the next 45 years. Some of his views were engraved as book illustrations; a moonlit view illustrated Sir Walter Scott's *Provincial Antiquities of Scotland* (1834). One of his most celebrated oils is of Norham Castle melting into the mist, an unfinished 'colour beginning' from the last years of his life (c 1844–50, Tate Collections).

Rising above the River Tweed, the 12th-century tower of Norham Castle still seems to guard the historic frontier between England and Scotland. Built in 1121 by Bishop Ranulph Flambard of Durham to protect and help administer his territories of Norhamshire and Islandshire against raiding Scots, the castle became redundant by the middle of the 16th century with the advancement of artillery and military architecture. The great gun ('bombard') Mons Meg, now in Edinburgh Castle, had inflicted considerable damage here when the Scots besieged Norham without success in 1497. The Great Tower was heightened in the 15th century to form a four-storey tower house providing high-quality lodgings, but by the end of the 16th century the castle had deteriorated and the constable lived in the Sheep Gate. When King James VI of Scotland became James I of England, after the death of Elizabeth I in 1603, the River Tweed had no need of military protection and the castle deteriorated.

Samuel and Nathaniel Buck published a prospect of the castle in 1728 with an inscription explaining how Ranulph, Bishop of Durham built it 'on the top of a steep rock … for the better security of this part of his Diocese against the frequent incursions of the Scotch Moss-Troopers'. The print is dedicated to the then owner of the castle, William Orde, but shows it in a ruinous state, with much of the earth banking in front of the walls removed.

The Bucks' engraving would have encouraged antiquarians to visit Norham Castle, but Sir Walter Scott's epic poem *Marmion* (1808) spread its appeal to a wider audience with its evocation of a world of chivalrous knights in the Borders. Scott drew on Thomas Gray's *Scalacronica* in telling how Sir William Marmion volunteered to serve at Norham – the most dangerous place in England – to prove his love for his mistress. Gray's father was constable of the castle and called on Marmion to ride out as knight errant to face the Scots, single-handed, which he did, until the constable and his garrison had to come to his rescue.

Thomas Allom (1804–72), *Norham Castle, on the Tweed, North Durham,* 1832, engraving (English Heritage)

J M W Turner (1775–1851), *Norham Castle*, 1824, watercolour (British Museum)

Okehampton Castle, Devon

To the painter Richard Wilson, who had been born in Wales, Okehampton could have carried historical associations as the home of the English oppressors from across the border. Wilson's painting in the Birmingham Museum & Art Gallery is probably the view of the castle he exhibited at the Royal Academy in 1774. He gives it an Italianate character, influenced by the paintings of the Italian countryside by Claude Lorrain and Gaspard Dughet, in seeing the castle from a distance in a broad panoramic setting that includes the town. Wilson's earlier view of the castle (1771–2) was probably painted for the then owner, William, 2nd Viscount Courtenay, to hang in his principal seat, Powderham Castle. This view would have appealed to a more romantic sensibility for it presents the castle from closer up, in silhouette, rising behind the River Okement, rather like a painting by the 17th-century Dutch master Jacob van Ruisdael.

When William the Conqueror appointed Baron Baldwin de Bionne as Sheriff of Devon to quell the threat of rebellion from the south-west he built his castle on high ground above the valley of the River Okement on a main route to Cornwall. Okehampton Castle was as much a symbol of the Normans' new dominance over the Saxons as an administrative centre. The choice of location may also have been commercial in order to develop a trade route, for the Domesday Book (1086) records here one of the only two markets in Devon, together with a mill and four free traders ('burgesses') in the new town of Okehampton. After Baldwin's death in 1090, two of his sons contributed to the conquest of South Wales.

Baldwin's descendants used the castle as a country retreat for entertaining – with a deer park for hunting – rather than as their main residence. The castle was rebuilt with luxurious lodgings to suit this purpose by Hugh Courtenay, 1st Earl of Devon in the 14th century. His descendants' long association with Okehampton ended in 1539 with the beheading of Henry Courtenay, 9th Earl of Devon, whom Henry VIII had created Marquess of Exeter. Local builders probably later helped themselves to the abandoned castle and it is recorded as a ruin in 1734 in an engraving by Samuel and Nathaniel Buck. The ruins of Okehampton had been leased for use as a bakehouse and watermill since 1682.

Richard Wilson (c 1713–82), *The Keep of Okehampton Castle, c* 1771–2, oil on canvas (Manchester Art Gallery)

Richard Wilson (*c* 1713–82), *Okehampton Castle*, *c* 1774, oil on canvas (Birmingham Museum & Art Gallery)

Old Sarum, Wiltshire

LIKE HIS TRAGIC VISION OF HADLEIGH CASTLE (exhibited at the Royal Academy in 1829, *see* p 61), Constable's view of Old Sarum is an expression of the grief he felt at the death of his wife Maria from tuberculosis in 1828. He exhibited this watercolour at the Royal Academy in 1834, the year he told a friend he felt hardly 'able to do any one thing' due to depression.

Constable described Old Sarum as 'wild, desolate and dreary', it was a subject 'which from its barren and deserted character seems to embody the words of the poet – "Paint me a desolation."' He felt 'the grander phenomena of Nature … thunderclouds, wild autumnal evenings, solemn and shadowy twilights' best suited it. The associations were also political. He wrote: 'This proud and "towered city", once giving laws to the whole kingdom – for it was here our earliest parliaments on record were convened – can now be traced but by vast embankments and ditches, tracked only by sheep-walks.'

The site of the ancient city of Salisbury, Old Sarum still rises high above Salisbury Plain today, with ruins of its own cathedral, castle, a royal palace, bishop's palace, cloister, earthworks and gates. Its name derives from the Celtic *Sorviadun* meaning 'the fortress by the gentle river'. The area was settled in prehistoric times and the original hillfort earthworks date from the Iron Age (700 BC–AD 43). Five Roman roads ran close to Old Sarum and it may have served travellers as a posting-station. The Saxons strengthened the fortress's earthworks to deter Viking raiders and then established a

mint to pay them off in *Danegeld*. In 1070 William the Conqueror chose Old Sarum as the setting for the mass demobilisation of his army, probably as so many roads converged nearby. Part of the Domesday Book was written here and, on its completion in 1086, all the principal landholders in England came to swear allegiance to William at Old Sarum. A new cathedral, built by Bishop Osmund, was consecrated in 1092; it was rebuilt and enlarged soon after 1100 and elaborate palaces were built for Bishop Roger and King Henry I.

As the town expanded the water supply proved insufficient. When the garrison and clergy finally fell out the bishop obtained the permission of Pope Honorius III to move the cathedral from the windy, rainswept hill shared with the soldiers to a new site, a meadow in a curve of the River Avon. Here in 1219 the bishop, as landowner, also obtained a market licence. By 1377 the population of Old Sarum had shrunk to ten taxpayers and by 1540 all the houses had gone. Nevertheless, until 1832 Old Sarum continued to 'elect' its own Member of Parliament, as a notorious 'rotten borough' in the control of its landowner. By the time Constable came to paint Old Sarum campaigners for the Great Reform Act of Parliament of 1832 had used it as an example of the need to reform the electoral system. In 1831 Constable expressed his fear that Reform would 'give the government into the hands of the rabble and dregs of the people, and the devil's agents on earth, the agitators'.

John Constable (1776–1837), *The Mound of the City of Old Sarum from the South*, 1834, watercolour (Victoria & Albert Museum)

Orford Castle, Suffolk

HENRY II CAME TO THE THRONE IN 1154. Not only was he King of England, but he also held the titles of Duke of Normandy and Aquitaine, Count of Anjou and Lord of Brittany. To consolidate his position in England he strengthened his major castles at Carlisle, Newcastle, Scarborough and Dover and also confiscated or destroyed several castles belonging to influential barons who posed a threat to his authority. Construction of Orford Castle was begun by Henry II in 1165, the same year he returned Framlingham Castle to Hugh Bigod, Earl of Norfolk, having confiscated it from him (along with three others) in 1157. The castle was quickly built, partly spurred on by Henry II's fear of a possible invasion after his quarrel with Thomas Becket, Archbishop of Canterbury, who had subsequently fled to France in 1164. The castle was completed in 1173 at a total cost of £1,413 – at a time when the king's average annual income was just over £18,000.

The distinctive polygonal keep, set within curtain walls, served not only as a symbol of the king's authority over East Anglia but also to defend the Suffolk coast against attack from France. The castle also played an important role in quashing the 1173–4 rebellion by Henry II's queen, Eleanor of Aquitaine, and their sons, which was supported by Hugh Bigod and the King of France.

Orford grew as a market town with shipping sheltering from the sea in Orford Ness, but by the early 14th century the estuary was silting up and, in 1336, King Edward III sold it to Robert of Ufford (the Younger), the future Earl of Suffolk. The castle declined from the 16th century as it became a source of building materials. It escaped bombardment and 'slighting' in the Civil War and survived as a landmark of interest to antiquarians and artists. The castle was also used as a navigational aid to shipping and this prevented its demolition in 1805. Its value as a seamark is clear from J M W Turner's view of c 1826, published in *Picturesque Views in England and Wales* (1825–38).

Henry Bright's view of 1856 shows Orford Castle and village from the south-west, with Orford Ness in the distance and the results of sand quarrying in the foreground. An exhibition reviewer praised it at the time for 'the fine aerial effects which make you feel as if you were actually abroad under the open canopy of heaven, inhaling the freshness and buoyancy of the breeze'.

In his autobiography the art historian – and former director of the National Gallery – Kenneth Clark fondly recalled visiting his grandmother at Castle House, which overlooked the castle, and later taking holidays in the nearby town of Aldeburgh, where he wrote several books. An image of the castle was used on a Shell petrol advertisement poster to entice people to explore this part of Suffolk.

J M W Turner (1775–1851), *Orford, c* 1826, engraving (Tate Collections)

Allan Walton (1892–1948), *Orford Castle. Everywhere You Go, You Can Be Sure of Shell*, 1932, poster (National Motor Museum, Beaulieu, Hampshire)

Henry Bright (c 1810–73), *Orford Castle*, 1856, oil on canvas (Norwich Castle Museum)

Osborne House, Isle of Wight

QUEEN VICTORIA AND PRINCE ALBERT built their ideal home, an Italianate marine villa overlooking the Solent from the north shore of the Isle of Wight, between 1845 and 1851. They were both in their mid-20s and needed somewhere private to raise a family that would grow to a total of 9 children (and 39 grandchildren). Their previous seaside home, Brighton Pavilion, had proved to be too exposed to the curiosity of the townsfolk. Nevertheless, Britain and its growing empire could not be left to run itself. For all its *gemütlichkeit* ('cosiness', a favourite word among the family who spoke German at home), the villa was outgrown by the buildings alongside, as they were built to accommodate the royal household and visiting ministers of government with their civil servants.

Osborne was designed by Prince Albert who chose to work with the builder Thomas Cubitt. The earliest views of the house show it under construction in a series of watercolours by William Leighton Leitch, who also taught Queen Victoria and her family to paint. Leitch's watercolour of 1847 shows the upper terrace in full bloom under blue skies. The views across to Portsmouth from the terraces almost live up to Prince Albert's comparison of the prospect with that of the Bay of Naples.

Public interest in the house soon spread and it was engraved as the title page illustration to Robert Kerr's *The Gentleman's House; or How to Plan English Residences, from the Parsonage to the Palace* (1864). Kerr also illustrated his text with complete plans of the ground floor of the 'Pavilion' and of the 'Apartments for Visitors', taken from the professional journal *The Builder*. The view painted by Thomas Allom, an architect who also specialised in such architectural 'perspectives', was probably commissioned to be engraved. Following Prince Albert's sudden death in December 1861, Queen Victoria went into mourning at Osborne. The house forms the background to her mourning portrait by Sir Edwin Landseer – *Sorrow*, also known as *Osborne, 1865* – which hangs in the Royal Collection at Osborne.

By 1890, the growing volume of visitors drawn from across the globe to Osborne necessitated the construction of the Durbar Wing for state receptions. Here Queen Victoria, as Empress of India, came as close as possible to the subcontinent without actually going there, by displaying her collection of Jubilee gifts from her loyal subjects in rooms designed by John Lockwood Kipling (father of Rudyard) and by a Sikh craftsman, Bhai Ram Singh. In 1904, three years after her death here, Osborne opened to the public. Ever popular, it is an early example of the 'country house tourism' that expanded rapidly after the Second World War.

Thomas Allom (1804–72), *Osborne House*, c 1850, line and wash (English Heritage, Osborne House)

William Leighton Leitch (1804–83), *Osborne House,
The Terraces under Construction*, 1847, watercolour
(Royal Collection)

William Leigton Leitch (1804–83),
The Pavilion, Osborne House, 1850,
watercolour (Royal Collection)

Pendennis Castle, Cornwall

THIS EXPANSIVE PROSPECT of the town, harbour, castles and shipping in the bay at the mouth of the River Fal probably belongs to the most important commission received by the painter Hendrick Danckerts, to paint 28 views of palaces and ports for Charles II, for whom he worked as Court Painter. It shows the deep port at peace – flourishing under the protection of its castles – with shipping and an almost Arcadian group of relaxed onlookers.

Henry VIII commissioned the construction of a pair of castles to guard the mouth of the Fal, one at St Mawes and the other at the top of the Pendennis Headland. With other artillery forts, such as those guarding Deal, Walmer and Yarmouth, Pendennis and St Mawes formed the most westerly link of a Tudor defensive chain constructed between 1540 and 1545 along the south coast of England to prevent the use of anchorages by enemy fleets. Surrounded by Elizabethan earthen ramparts (commissioned 1598–1600), Pendennis was the larger of the two castles. Today the site covers two acres and also includes a storehouse built during the French Revolutionary and Napoleonic Wars (1793–1815) and a barrack block that was completed in 1902.

In the early 16th century this remote part of Cornwall was still almost a different country. When in 1506 a ship carrying Philip of Burgundy sought shelter in the River Fal estuary a fellow passenger, the Venetian Ambassador to Castile, wrote of it as a 'very wild place, which no human being ever visits … in the midst of a barbarous race' whose Cornish language was unintelligible to the English. The need to build forts here came in 1530 when, after Henry VIII declared himself supreme head of the Church of England, Spain and France signed a treaty and agreed to form a navy to invade England and re-establish the authority of the Papacy. Henry proudly referred to all his new forts as castles, despite the fact that they were strictly utilitarian buildings to house guns and gunners, not ostentatious residences of land owners.

Pendennis fought off Spanish fleets in 1588 and 1597. During the Civil War it was occupied by Royalist forces and, in the siege of 1646, 1,000 men held out for five months before surrendering to the Parliamentarians. Prince Charles, later King Charles II, had stayed at Pendennis in March 1646 before escaping by sea to the Scilly Isles. Two years earlier his mother, Queen Henrietta Maria, had sailed from Pendennis to France. These Royalist associations would have added to the significance of Pendennis after the Restoration in 1660 and may have led to the commission for Danckerts' painting of 1678.

Over the next 10 years Falmouth became a principal base for the packet boats, which carried mail and passengers to destinations around the world. The packet trade continued until the 1830s. In J M W Turner's painting (engraved in 1817 for *Picturesque Views on the Southern Coast of England*) he captures the turbulent condition of the wild sea with a scene of shipwreck victims struggling ashore.

After the First World War both Pendennis and St Mawes opened to the public and became familiar landmarks to ramblers, before being recommissioned along with many historic fortresses along the south coast at the start of the Second World War. Falmouth Bay became the first port of call for ships crossing the Atlantic. From 1942 Falmouth became so full of US servicemen that it became known as the 49th State. The army finally moved out of Pendennis Castle in 1956.

J M W Turner (1775–1851), *Pendennis Castle and Entrance to Falmouth Harbour, Cornwall* (from *Picturesque Views on the Southern Coast of England*), 1817, intaglio print on paper (Tate Collections)

Hendrick Danckerts (c 1625–90), *A View of Falmouth Harbour*, 1678, oil on canvas (National Maritime Museum)

Pevensey Castle, East Sussex

JOHN HAMILTON MORTIMER FILLS HIS CANVAS with the massive remains of Pevensey's gatehouse, gnawed by tempest and time on the windswept East Sussex coast. His low, close-up viewpoint sets the towers against the stormy sky almost as if they could collapse on our heads. A maid carrying a jug adds to the sense of scale and a struggling silver birch tree recoils from the ruin, but these picturesque conventions only highlight the savaged state of the castle in this essay in the Sublime. The castle's Roman ingredients would have enriched its melancholy appeal as a reminder of the futility of human endeavour. By contrast, Michael Angelo Rooker finds a quieter, more sheltered corner in the inner bailey to paint beneath the South Tower, where a hole in the wall is not a void but rather frames a smooth landscape complete with hayricks.

William the Conqueror landed at Pevensey on 28 September 1066 and his troops spent their first night in the Roman fort on the site, then known as *Anderida*. The next day they marched to face King Harold's army near Hastings. After the conquest, his troops returned. Roman walls were retained when the stone keep was built around 1100 and when the curtain wall, towers and gatehouse were added in the 13th century. The final inhabitants included King James I and the stepmother of King Henry V, Joan of Navarre, when it served as a state prison in the 15th century. By the time Samuel and Nathaniel Buck published their engraved view of Pevensey in 1737, the castle had been a ruin for two centuries. Pevensey was expected to see action again in the Second World War when pillboxes for machine gun posts were built in the ruins, constructed in matching materials as camouflage, where they remain today.

Michael Angelo Rooker (1746–1801), *Ruins of Pevensey Castle, c* 1780, pencil and watercolour (Victoria & Albert Museum)

John Hamilton Mortimer (1741–79), *A View of The West Gate of Pevensey Castle, Sussex, c* 1774, oil on canvas (Yale Center for British Art, Paul Mellon Fund, USA)

Ranger's House, London

FACING BLACKHEATH FROM THE WALL OF GREENWICH PARK, a short walk from the Royal Observatory, Ranger's House is the first house in the world on the line of the Greenwich Meridian. Standing in the dining room, one may straddle 0 degrees longitude, the first meridian line around the globe. This unique location would have appealed to Admiral Francis Hosier (b 1673), who built the house by 1700 (when his name first appears in local rate books). His naval salary alone could not have financed the villa and he must have made his fortune from prize money from captured ships and from his shares in the South Sea Company. One may imagine him on the house's flat balustraded roof at night, high above Greenwich and London, charting the stars with his sextant, as if on the deck of a ship. He died at sea in 1727.

The villa first attracted public interest after it became the fashionable retreat of Philip Dormer Stanhope, 4th Earl of Chesterfield, in the 18th century. The great diplomat inherited the house from his brother in 1748; he preferred to live in Mayfair but gradually retired to Blackheath where he wrote many of his celebrated letters to his natural son, Philip. They were first published in 1774, by his son's widow, and became a bestseller as an essential handbook on self-advancement in society. Dr Johnson said they taught 'the morals of a whore and the manners of a dancing-master'. A Japanese translation is still selling well today.

The first engraving of the house appeared in *The Lady's Magazine* in 1808 when it was the home of King George III's sister, the Dowager Duchess of Brunswick. She came to live at Chesterfield House (as it was then known) to be near her daughter, Caroline, Princess of Wales, who lived next door following her separation from her husband, the future George IV. In 1815 Princess Sophia Matilda, niece of George III, became the first Ranger of Greenwich Park to live at the house. Her death in 1844 prompted several engravings in the illustrated press showing her lying-in-state and her funeral procession leaving the house.

The only known oil painting of the house was commissioned by Blanche, Countess of Mayo, who lived at Chesterfield House from 1876 following the assassination of her husband, the Viceroy and Governor-General of India. Anthony de Bree's painting gives prominence, on the right, to the long gallery, added by the 4th Earl of Chesterfield. As he wrote in 1750: 'The shell of my gallery is finished, which, by three bow-windows, gives me three different, and the finest, prospects in the world.' The gallery still faces the royal park of Greenwich, Blackheath and its own walled garden. On the left, the painting shows the cupola and weather vane on the former stables (only the cupola survives) and a street lamp on Chesterfield Walk. It also reveals the former covered entrance between the public path and the front door that was built to afford Princess Sophia greater privacy. A Dutch painter, de Bree was discovered, living in poverty, by the Earl of Mayo who commissioned him to paint copies of his pictures; he also worked for King Edward VII as a copyist.

In 1902 the house was purchased by London County Council who opened it the following year as changing rooms for sports clubs using Blackheath and as a tea room. It was first restored as a museum and gallery in 1960. Since 2002 Ranger's House has been the permanent home of the Wernher Collection of Renaissance art, formed by Julius Wernher, a founder of the diamond miners De Beers.

Anonymous, *The Funeral Procession of Princess Sophia Leaving Her House*, 1844, lithograph published in *The Pictorial Times* (Greenwich Local History Library)

Anthony de Bree (fl 1882–1913), *Chesterfield House, Blackheath*, 1884, oil on canvas (Museum of London)

Richmond Castle, North Yorkshire

THIS IDYLLIC PROSPECT OF RICHMOND IN NORTH YORKSHIRE, crowned by its castle, was painted by the Dutch artist Alexander Keirincx, probably when he visited England from Amsterdam in 1640–1 to paint views of royal castles and palaces for King Charles I. The topographical record is enhanced by the panoramic setting, radiant lime green hills, cloudy blue sky and the valley of the River Swale. The foreground foliage screens the scene from picturesque travellers.

This serene spectacle by Keirincx seems worlds away from a medieval drawing of the castle, seen from the north, preserved in an early 15th-century register of documents relating to the Honour of Richmond, a vast estate spread over eight counties. It illustrates the records of 'knight service' owed by generations of landholders to their feudal overlord and attempts to show the castle buildings as they would have appeared in the 1190s, each annotated with the coats of arms of the knight responsible for providing garrison troops.

Richmond Castle was probably established in the 1070s by Alan Rufus, Count of Penthièvre in Brittany, to defend the estates he had received from his uncle, William the Conqueror, against their former owners among the Anglo-Saxon nobility. It remains the largest and best preserved 11th-century castle in England but has been in a ruinous state since the 14th century when it passed by inheritance to the Dukes of Brittany. A condition of inheritance was obedience to the King of England, which led to its confiscation by the Crown on several occasions. The existence of Keirincx's painting suggests that Charles I may have considered Richmond to be his own.

Unknown scribe, *Richmond Castle in the 1190s*, 15th century, coloured drawing (British Library)

Alexander Keirincx (1600–*c* 1652), *Richmond Castle, Yorkshire, c* 1640–1, oil on panel (Yale Center for British Art, Paul Mellon Fund, USA)

Rievaulx Abbey, North Yorkshire

THE CISTERCIAN MONKS who came from Clairvaux in France in 1132 chose the beautiful deserted valley of the River Rye among the Yorkshire hills as a suitable setting for their monastery. Rievaulx Abbey flourished for 400 years and grew into the foremost Cistercian monastery in Britain. The third abbot, Aelred (1110–67), became the most prominent religious figure in the country at the head of the largest monastic establishment. Canonised in Rome, St Aelred was the subject of a biography written at Rievaulx and, in the 13th century, his body was moved to a gold and silver shrine behind the high altar in a new presbytery. In 1538 the monastery surrendered to the authority of Henry VIII who granted it, with its estates, to Thomas Manners, Earl of Rutland; the systematic destruction of its 72 buildings then followed.

The ruins of Rievaulx Abbey became a picturesque feature of the gardens of Duncombe Park in 1758 when Thomas Duncombe chose them as the focus of a carefully planned landscape walk with temples along the hillside above, a path over half a mile long now known as Rievaulx Terrace. An Ionic temple was designed as a banqueting house where his guests could dine and enjoy vistas across to Ryedale and the Hambleton Hills. The house stands about three miles away from the ruins and the hunting party painted by John Wootton around 1728 is made up of guests of the Duncombe family. In this lively scene the four riders converse with a shepherd while a group of labourers, perhaps stonemasons, use a ladder to make repairs. Grassy mounds reveal the presence of architectural debris, long overgrown, still lying where it had fallen centuries earlier. The sporting artist painted another view of the abbey (unlocated) which was recorded hanging in the Saloon at Duncombe Park in 1812.

As a ruin Rievaulx became popular with writers and artists in the age of Romanticism. Dorothy Wordsworth found at Rievaulx: 'Green hillocks among the ruins … [and] wild roses. I could have stayed in this solemn spot 'til evening.' Thomas Girtin, John Sell Cotman and Paul Sandby Munn painted Rievaulx between 1798 and 1806. J M W Turner sketched here in 1801 and his 1827 view of the abbey is the first plate in *Picturesque Views*

in England and Wales (1825–38). William Westall and Copley Fielding also painted Rievaulx in the 1820s and 1830s. The pioneer photographer Roger Fenton came in 1854 (*see* p 6).

Rievaulx escaped archaeological excavation until 1919. In 1913 Ancient Monuments Protection legislation had been passed that enabled the state to take into its care monuments of national significance. As part of the consolidation of the monument, excavations proceeded after the First World War with the help of demobbed soldiers. Fred Taylor's poster for the London & North Eastern Railway, issued to draw travellers to the local station at Helmsley, shows tempting young ladies lounging among Rievaulx's ruins, with the caption 'Recently Excavated Chapter House in Foreground'. Edwin Byatt's view (*see* p 7) was painted for reproduction as prints that hung beneath the luggage racks in railway carriages.

Fred Taylor (1875–1963), *Rievaulx Abbey, Helmsley, Yorks, c* 1933, poster (National Railway Museum)

John Wootton (1682–1764),
*A Hunting Party by the Ruins of
Rievaulx Abbey, c* 1728, oil on canvas
(Yale Center for British Art, Paul
Mellon Collection, USA)

Scarborough Castle, North Yorkshire

JAMES GREEN'S HUMOROUS SCENE OF REGENCY SOCIETY attempting to promenade on the Spa Terrace was published to illustrate his *Poetical Sketches of Scarborough* (1813). The title is clearly intended as an ironic response to the more precious picturesque folios then becoming fashionable in polite circles. Windswept young ladies struggle to preserve their modesty from the gaze of soldiers on leave from the castle in the background. In another view by the artist a lady's parasol is blown away after a visit to the castle in an episode worthy of Jane Austen.

Seafaring raiders from the north were among the first visitors to the bay now lined by the resort town of Scarborough. The danger presented by these raiders prompted the construction of a signal station by the Romans around AD 370 on the headland north of the bay, where its remains survive next to the castle. Vikings settled here in the 10th century. In the 12th century Henry II recognised that the promontory, connected to the mainland by a neck of land and surrounded by cliffs, formed a natural fortress from which to defend the harbour and Scarborough was strengthened to become a royal powerbase in Yorkshire.

Mineral springs were discovered here in the 1620s and, in the 18th century, the town developed as a fashionable spa. It grew in Victorian times as a holiday resort in response to the new pastime of sea bathing. Scarborough was also a favoured haunt of smugglers.

As the flag flying above the walls in Green's view of the castle indicates, it was no deserted picturesque ruin. Two sieges in 1645 during the Civil War had done so much damage that the order to 'slight' the castle had been ignored. Nevertheless, it survived as a prison and in 1746, a year after the Jacobite Rebellion, a barrack was built to house 120 officers and men. The garrison was re-established in response to the French Revolutionary and Napoleonic Wars and troops continued to be stationed on the headland until the late 19th century. By the time the London & North Eastern Railway published their posters to entice travellers back to Scarborough's golden sands (*see* p 7), the town and castle had suffered from bombardment in December 1914 by German battle cruisers.

Thomas Rowlandson (1756–1827)
after James Green (1771–1834),
The Castle, 1813, chromolithograph
(British Library)

Joseph Constantine Sadler (fl 1780–1812) after James Green (1771–1834), *Scarborough Castle from the Spa Terrace*, 1813, chromolithograph (British Library)

St Mawes Castle, Cornwall

IN THE PAINTING BY J M W TURNER, fishermen shovel pilchards into baskets and barrels on the shore, safe beneath the protection of the castles of Pendennis and St Mawes, which guard the mouth of the Fal estuary. This sense of the English as an industrious island race who have made the most of the sea is also conveyed by an oil painting, *St Mawes at the Pilchard Season* (Tate Collections), which Turner exhibited in his own gallery in 1812, when the country was still at war with Napoleonic France.

St Mawes is the smaller of the two artillery forts built in Falmouth Bay between 1540 and 1543 as part of a chain around the south of England, following Henry VIII's break with the Roman Catholic Church and his Dissolution of the monasteries. The clover-leaf plan of three interlocked round towers was revolutionary at the time. It provided gun platforms above thick curved walls that could deflect cannon balls fired from enemy ships and these forts were also difficult to hit due to their low profile against the skyline. Unfortunately, Pendennis and St Mawes were not designed to withstand siege from the land and in the Civil War the Royalist governors surrendered to Parliamentarian forces.

As the most westerly safe anchorage in the British Channel, the estuary between the castles became an assembly point for British naval squadrons from the 16th century and, in the 17th century, ships would leave from here carrying paying passengers and mail to Ireland and the Continent, and later to the Americas and East Indies. During the Civil War, Queen Henrietta Maria came here to sail for France in 1644 and two years later her son Charles (later Charles II) escaped from here to the Scilly Isles, and then to Jersey.

From 1572 until the Reform Bill of 1832 the St Mawes garrison elected its own Member of Parliament. With between 16 and 100 men it was not so notorious a 'rotten borough' as the deserted town of Old Sarum (*see* p 92) but the castle governor expected to be elected.

St Mawes saw service in the Second World War as a barrage balloon station, with a new gun battery, to help defend the docks at Falmouth from German air raids. St Mawes and Pendennis finally returned to the care of the Ministry of Works (the predecessor of English Heritage) when the Coastal Artillery Branch of the army was disbanded in 1956.

J M W Turner (1775–1851), *St Mawes, Cornwall*, *c* 1822, watercolour with scratching out (Yale Center for British Art, Paul Mellon Collection, USA)

Stokesay Castle, Shropshire

LAWRENCE OF LUDLOW, an international wool merchant based in Shrewsbury, had bought the tenancy of Stokesay in 1281 for the price of a 'juvenile sparrow hawk'. He was probably the leading wool merchant in England and must have aspired to join the gentry for he began building an imposing manor house soon after 1281. Encircled by a water-filled moat it combined a great hall and comfortable private apartment with two defensive towers. In 1291 he obtained a 'licence to crenellate' from Edward I, enabling him to add defensive battlements. However, Stokesay was not called a castle until the 16th century. The elaborately carved half-timbered gatehouse and half-timbering on the north tower were added in the 17th century.

Stokesay opened to the public in 1908 after half a century of sympatheic repairs by its owners, the Allcroft family. The importance of the late 13th-century fortified manor house as a rare architectural survivor had long been recognised. John Britton had included it in *The Architectural Antiquities of Great Britain* (1814) and Stokesay was illustrated in T H Turner's *Some Account of Domestic Architecture in England* (1851), where it was described as 'one of the most perfect and interesting thirteenth century buildings which we possess'. In his *Castles and Abbeys* (1877) the American novelist Henry James relished at Stokesay 'the sensation of dropping back personally into the past … while I lay on the grass beside the well in the little sunny court of this small castle'. Thanks to its complete preservation he 'lazily appreciated the still definite details of medieval life. The place is a capital example of a small *gentilhommière* of the thirteenth century'.

David Cox's watercolour of the exterior of the west range shows the main front of the castle facing the road from Ludlow in the foreground with the battlements of the south tower silhouetted beyond. In John Piper's more frontal view from the road, the ancient manor house takes on a life of its own and seems almost surreal in its eerie, uneven silhouette, stretched recumbent like some great slumbering beast. At this time Stokesay Castle still belonged to Lady Allcroft; it only came into the care of English Heritage in 1992.

John Piper (1903–92), *Stokesay Castle*, 1981, watercolour and mixed media (Private Collection)

David Cox (1783–1859), *Stokesay Castle and Abbey*, *c* 1820, watercolour (Private Collection)

Stonehenge, Wiltshire

WHEN JOHN CONSTABLE'S WATERCOLOUR OF STONEHENGE was shown at the Royal Academy in 1836 the exhibition catalogue included the following lines, presumably written by the artist himself:

The mysterious monument of Stonehenge, standing remote on a bare and boundless heath, as much unconnected with the events of past ages as it is with the uses of the present, carries you back beyond all historical records into the obscurity of a totally unknown period.

Nearly two centuries later, our knowledge of Stonehenge's origins have improved considerably, but our understanding of the spirit of the people who created it, as Constable seems to capture, is no less mysterious.

Constable's only known visit to Stonehenge was on 15 July 1820 when he made a detailed tonal drawing on which this watercolour is based. The seated shepherd, admiring antiquarians and a distant wagon drawn by horses all appear in both, but the watercolour alone has the dramatic storm clouds, faint double rainbow and a hare running out of the foreground. This contrast between the heavy permanence of the megaliths and these fleeting elements suggests that time was weighing on his mind. Constable painted *Stonehenge* in early September 1835; the previous month his son Charles had joined an East Indiaman as a midshipman, at his father's suggestion, and was not to return until a year later, when they met for the last time.

Constable may also have been responding to J M W Turner's bleak image of Stonehenge in a thunderstorm (Salisbury and South Wiltshire Museum), which had been exhibited in London and published in 1829. Of another painting by Turner shown at the Royal Academy in 1836, Constable wrote: 'Turner has outdone himself – he seems to paint with tinted steam, so evanescent, and so airy.' The hare in Constable's *Stonehenge* is a late addition, on a separate piece of paper pasted on, and may have been a response to Turner's painting at the Academy exhibition. Constable died the following year.

The moonlit views by Edward McKnight Kauffer and John Piper (*see* p 9) make the megaliths seem even more mysterious and imposing by taking closer, lower viewpoints. Kauffer's poster for Shell petrol would have appealed to motor car drivers using the main road (A303) in 1931, for whom Stonehenge became a familiar landmark as the gateway to the west country.

The most important prehistoric monument in Britain, Stonehenge was begun around 3100 BC. The present structure was assembled about 2000 BC using sarsen blocks from the Marlborough Downs, with bluestones from the Preseli Mountains in south-west Wales arranged within the circle. It was originally entered from a processional route aligned with the midsummer sunrise. When viewed from the centre of the circle the midsummer sun passes above the Heel Stone. The 17th-century antiquary John Aubrey (who discovered and surveyed Avebury) first suggested that the Druids built Stonehenge, but this Celtic priesthood dates from the Iron Age. For all its fame, Stonehenge was privately owned until 1918 when it was given to the nation.

Edward McKnight Kauffer (1890–1954), *Stonehenge: See Britain First on Shell*, 1931, poster (National Motor Museum, Beaulieu, Hampshire)

John Constable (1776–1837), *Stonehenge*, 1835–6, watercolour (Victoria & Albert Museum)

Tilbury Fort, Essex

TILBURY FORT was one of five small forts on the River Thames built for Henry VIII in 1539 as part of his coastal defence scheme. These forts guarded the mouth of the River Thames, which led to arsenals and dockyards at Woolwich and Deptford. Most had deteriorated by 1558 when Elizabeth I came to the throne but the ones at West Tilbury and Gravesend were repaired to face the Spanish Armada in 1588. Under the command of the Earl of Leicester, 17,000 men were mustered at Tilbury to face a Spanish landing force of 20,000, with a further 17,000 ready to cross from the Netherlands. Leicester invited Elizabeth to visit and address them 'to comfort not only these thousands but many more that shall hear of it'.

This 17th-century painting shows her arrival on a white horse on 8 August in the great procession of 1,000 men on horseback and 2,000 on foot that escorted her from her barge to the camp on the hill by Tilbury church. The same day the two fleets engaged off Gravelines, as shown in the background. The 90 English ships under Lord Howard succeeded in dispersing the Armada to the north and bad weather did the rest. The painting presents the two events as directly linked, as they were seen at the time, as a Protestant English triumph over Catholic Spain, thanks to divine intervention. The text painted beneath the scene quotes Elizabeth's address to the troops on 9 August, which includes the stirring declaration: ' I know I have but the body of a weak and feeble woman; but I have the heart and stomach of a king, and of a king of England too.'

In 1605 the defeat of the Gunpowder Plot was seen as another sign of Protestant England's divine protection. The other half of this painting,

William Clarkson Stanfield (1793–1867), *Tilbury Fort. Wind Against the Tide*, 1853, oil on canvas (Yale Center for British Art, Paul Mellon Collection, USA)

on two linked panels (a diptych) shows the trial of Guy Fawkes and his fellow conspirators. The diptych is traditionally said to have been donated to St Faith's Church, Gaywood, near King's Lynn, by its rector in the early 17th century.

The year after the Armada, an Italian engineer supervised the construction of fortified earthworks in the marshland around Tilbury's Tudor blockhouse. These were strengthened to a new design based on Dutch town and fort defences after the Restoration of Charles II in 1660. A new fort was commissioned in 1670 after the Dutch fleet attacked the English fleet at Chatham and made off with the flagship, the *Royal Charles* (part of which survives in the Rijksmuseum today). The monumental stone Water Gate was completed around 1682 and forms an impressive landmark for river traffic. In his view of 1853 the marine painter William Clarkson Stanfield has the gate catch the sunlight and shine out from the low-lying buildings at the mouth of the Thames, where the river begins to mix with the choppier open waters of the North Sea. Tilbury remains today the most complete example in Britain of a 17th-century bastioned artillery fort with outer defences.

As with many of England's castles in peacetime, Tilbury served as a prison. Jacobite supporters of the failed rebellion of 1745 were shipped from Inverness to Tilbury and those who survived were either executed after trial or transported to work as slaves in sugar plantations in Barbados and Antigua. With the advance of rifled artillery and steam-driven ironclad warships Tilbury was rearmed between 1868 and 1871 but again soon became obsolete. In the First World War it served as an ordnance depot; it remained in military use until 1950.

English School, Detail from *The Arrival of Queen Elizabeth I at Tilbury*, 17th century, oil on panel (St Faith's Church, Gaywood, Norfolk)

Tintagel Castle, Cornwall

JUTTING INTO THE ATLANTIC from the rocky coast of north Cornwall, the windswept headland of Tintagel has been a place of legend for centuries. Was this the birthplace of King Arthur, ruler of Camelot and leader of the Knights of the Round Table? Geoffrey of Monmouth would have us believe Arthur was conceived here. According to his *History of the Kings of Britain* (1136) Uther Pendragon used Merlin's magic to seduce Queen Igraine at Tintagel.

When Richard, Earl of Cornwall, brother of King Henry III, came to Tintagel in 1233 to build a castle on the island, he must have hoped to impress the Cornish as a worthy successor to King Arthur, for the strategic benefit of the site can only have been symbolic. Ambitious to be crowned Holy Roman Emperor, Richard also needed the support of kings and princes abroad, to whom the legend of Arthur would have appealed. After his death, later earls had little use for the remote castle, but when the first large-scale map of Cornwall was published in 1699 'King Arthur's Castle' was clearly marked.

Antiquarians, artists and other admirers came to Tintagel in increasing numbers in the 18th century. Samuel and Nathaniel Buck produced an engraving in 1734 and J M W Turner's watercolour (Museum of Fine Arts, Boston, Massachusetts, USA) was published in 1818. In Samuel Palmer's painting the ravaged remains of a castle just break the skyline above a cove where, opposite the dark mouth of Merlin's Cave, a mast is washed up on the shore from a shipwreck and a wagon trundles away laden with a vast anchor and chain. Victorian writers also came for inspiration, most notably Charles Dickens, Alfred, Lord Tennyson and Algernon Charles Swinburne. In *Idylls of the King* (1859), a popular narrative poem about King Arthur and his court, Tennyson pictures Merlin discovering Arthur as a baby in a cave by the shore. Thomas Hardy drew an 'Imaginary View of Tintagel Castle' for the frontispiece of his *Tragedy of the Queen of Cornwall* (1923).

To meet and increase tourist demand, the local village campaigned to get a railway branch line laid, to no avail, but did end up with a grand terminus hotel, modestly named King Arthur's Castle Hotel (it still stands on a nearby clifftop). In 1900 the village succeeded in changing its name from Trevena to Tintagel.

The Arthurian legend began to be taken more seriously after 1929 when the care of Tintagel passed to the government's Office of Works. Archaeologists made the first of a series of discoveries of pottery and glass from Spain, North Africa and the Eastern Mediterranean. Bernard Sleigh's woodcut of the ruins themselves, made in 1934, must have been prompted by the excavations when many buildings from the 'Dark Ages' were uncovered. At first these discoveries were explained as evidence of an early Christian monastery, but in 1986 new research was published that established the existence of a royal stronghold here in the 5th and 6th centuries AD. The most intriguing evidence came in 1998 with the discovery of a slate slab covering a 6th-century drain. It carries the name 'Artognov', which would have been pronounced 'Arthnou'. Either Richard, Earl of Cornwall was not the first to identify with the island's legendary associations – or Geoffrey of Monmouth was right.

Bernard Sleigh (1872–1954), *Tintagel*, 1934, woodcut (Cheltenham Art Gallery & Museum)

Samuel Palmer (1805–81), *Tintagel Castle. Approaching Rain*, 1848–9, watercolour (Ashmolean Museum, Oxford)

Upnor Castle, Kent

IN HENRY VIII's reign the upper reaches of the River Medway provided ideal anchorage for ships from his navy when not in service or when they were undergoing repairs. The dry docks at Chatham were not built until the reign of James I and by 1564 most of the fleet – 23 of the largest ships – was moored below Rochester Bridge. As Rochester Castle had been designed to guard the bridge, not ships, the fleet was vulnerable to raiders. Upnor Castle was built on the orders of Queen Elizabeth I between 1559 (the year she was crowned) and 1564. Despite its name it was a blockhouse, a utilitarian building to guard the River Medway, not the seat of a local lord.

William Hogarth's original view of Upnor Castle is one of nine drawings bound together with a manuscript in the British Museum. This illustrated journal is the graphic account of 'The Five Days Peregrination' from 27 May 1732 of five drinking partners. William Hogarth, his brother-in-law John Thornhill, the marine painter Samuel Scott, a lawyer named Ebenezer Forrest and William Tothall, a draper, travelled from London into north Kent by land and water. On the second night after their return the swiftly bound manuscript was read out at the Bedford Coffee House. Hogarth's view of 'Upner Castle' [sic] shows Scott sketching and Hogarth pointing. Forrest described the same scene:

I went and bought Cockles of an Old Blind Man and half Blind Woman who were in a Litle cock Boat on the River. Wee made a Hurry scurry Dinner at the Smack at ye Ten Gun Battery and had a Batle Royall with Sticks pebbles and Hog's Dung, in this Fight Tothall was the Greatest Sufferer and his Cloaths carried the Marks of his Disgrace some time, this occasion'd Much Laughter.

They continued on to 'Hoo Church yard':

Hogarth having a Motion; untruss'd upon a Grave rail in an unseemly Manner which Tothall Perceiving administred pennance to ye part offending with a Bunch of Netles, this occasion'd an Engagement which Ended hapily without Bloodshed and Hogarth Finish'd his Business against the Church Door.

The journal was published in facsimile in 1781 (as illustrated opposite). The excursion could be seen as a spoof of the Grand Tour of Europe by the aristocracy. Hogarth was a passionate advocate of English middle-class values and 'plain speaking'. At the time of the Peregrination's publication, Upnor Castle still carried painful memories of a national disgrace. The castle did not see action in defence of the fleet until 1667. Following victory at sea that year against the Dutch the English fleet was moored in the River Medway. On 12 June 1667 a Dutch squadron broke through the defences, set ships on fire and sailed off with the flagship, the *Royal Charles*, while the battery at Upnor blazed away. When the diarist John Evelyn visited Chatham he described the burnt hulks as 'a Dreadful Spectacle as ever any English men saw and a dishonour never to be wiped off'.

The following year Upnor Castle was downgraded to a store for weapons and gunpowder while new forts were built to defend the river. Thousands of barrels of gunpowder were stored here, far more than anywhere else in the country. With its own governor and garrison, Upnor continued as a powder magazine until 1827 when it became an Ordnance Laboratory. Prison hulks, as shown in the views by Hogarth and Thomas Rowlandson, and in a painting of Upnor by J M W Turner (Whitworth Art Gallery) continued to be moored here until the mid-19th century. In 1891 Upnor transferred to the Admiralty and gradually became a museum.

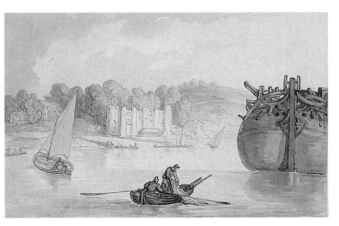

Thomas Rowlandson (1756–1827), *The River Medway at Upnor Castle*, 1790s, watercolour (Private Collection)

After William Hogarth (1697–1764) and Samuel Scott (*c* 1702–72), *The Castle of Upnor*, 1781, sepia etching (British Library)

Walmer Castle, Kent

THIS EARLY 18TH-CENTURY PROSPECT of three forts along the Kent coast has always hung above the mantelpiece in the dining room at Walmer Castle. It may have been commissioned by Lionel Sackville, 1st Duke of Dorset, to commemorate his appointment in 1708 as Lord Warden of the Cinque Ports. He was the first holder of the title to make Walmer Castle his official residence. The position had been created in the 13th century to coordinate and defend the ports of Dover, Hastings, Sandwich, Romney and Hythe. This view, in the style of the marine painter Willem van de Velde the Younger (1633–1707), shows Walmer, Deal and Sandown castles. It must date from after 1707 when England and Scotland agreed to share their sovereign and parliament under the Act of Union for Deal Castle flies the Union flag. The painting appears to record an official visit by either Queen Anne (d 1714) or by King George I, for the royal flagship is moored and firing a salute as a small ferryboat heads for shore.

Like Pendennis, St Mawes, Deal, Portland, Yarmouth and other artillery forts built for Henry VIII from 1539, Walmer Castle linked a defensive chain around the south coast of England that was created in readiness for an invasion by the combined forces of Catholic France and Spain, following the king's break with the spiritual authority of Rome.

The Duke of Wellington was appointed Lord Warden in 1829. As the liberator of Europe from Napoleon, Wellington was expected by a grateful nation to live in a vast new Waterloo Palace, but instead he kept the estate that was bought to be its setting, Stratfield Saye, and here his wife made her home. Wellington conducted his public and working life from Apsley House in London (*see* p 12) while he pursued a second career as a politician, but he was grateful to be appointed Master of the Cinque Ports as the position brought with it the use of Walmer Castle, where he could enjoy a relative degree of privacy.

When he died at Walmer Castle on 14 September 1852 the nation mourned and images of the Henrician fort on the Kent coast appeared in the popular press. Wellington's body lay in state at Walmer for two months before his funeral in St Paul's Cathedral and nearly 9,000 came to pay their respects in the final two days before his remains began their journey to London. The following year a chromolithograph of the room in which he died was published with a vivid description of every detail by Richard Ford in *Apsley House and Walmer Castle*. In 1934 the room was recreated as part of a Wellington Museum of memorablilia at Walmer Castle.

Other distinguished Lord Wardens include William Pitt the Younger (Lord Warden 1792–1805), Marquess Curzon of Kedleston (appointed 1904), Sir Winston Churchill (appointed 1941) and H M Queen Elizabeth the Queen Mother (appointed 1978). The painting of the three forts is protected by an Indenture of Heirlooms Act of Parliament initiated by W H Smith, who was Lord Warden in 1891.

Anonymous, *Mourners on the Beach below Walmer Castle*, 1852, illustration from *The Illustrated London News*, 20 November 1852

Unknown artist, *The Cinque Ports Castles of Walmer, Deal and Sandown*, early 18th century, oil on canvas (English Heritage, Walmer Castle)

Warkworth Castle, Northumberland

WHEN J M W TURNER EXHIBITED THIS WATERCOLOUR at the Royal Academy in 1799 he was an ambitious young man, aged 24, out to make his mark. The choice of subject seems particularly appropriate. This is no routine topographical study for reproduction as an illustration but is rather a complex and highly finished work that could outshine oil paintings at public exhibition. Turner based it on sketches he made on a tour of Yorkshire and Northumberland in 1797, when he also drew Dunstanburgh, Norham and other castles. The title he gave it for exhibition adds to the sense of being in the scene as the storm approaches. Turner also included in the exhibition catalogue the following lines from the poem *The Seasons* (1726–30) by James Thomson:

Behold slow settling o'er the lurid grove,
Unusual darkness broods; and growing, gains
The full possession of the sky; and on yon baleful cloud
A redd'ning gloom, a magazine of fate,
Ferment.

In the 16th century the Earls of Northumberland established their seat at Alnwick Castle, but Warkworth still carried romantic associations as the home of Harry Hotspur, Sir Henry Percy, heroic son of the first Earl of Northumberland, who was immortalised by Shakespeare in his play *Henry IV*. Hotspur and his father failed in their bid to overthrow Henry IV and Hotspur died in battle in 1403.

When King James I and his court visited Warkworth in 1617 goats and sheep lived everywhere on the site. The keep served as a store for oats from local estates and as somewhere to hold manorial courts. In 1648, during the Civil War, a Parliamentary garrison helped the castle's decline into a ruin and in 1672 it was stripped of lead and timber for building materials. In the 1850s the 4th Duke of Northumberland employed the architect Anthony Salvin to re-roof and refurbish the keep so that he could entertain his friends when out riding from Alnwick Castle. The gatehouse was also restored to accommodate the resident guide.

In a secluded setting on the north bank of the River Coquet some half a mile from the castle stands Warkworth Hermitage. The chapel and chambers were rough-hewn in the rock between the 14th and 16th centuries. Its appeal to the traveller in pursuit of the Picturesque is captured in S M Byron's watercolour of 1779 showing a group evidently encountering the hermit. A succession of hermits was supported by the lords of Warkworth. Initially their job was to pray for Christian salvation, but by the 1530s the 'hermit' drew a substantial salary, received fish and firewood and could pasture livestock. In return he was expected to manage the Warkworth estate for the 6th Earl of Northumberland.

S M Byron (fl 1779), *Warkworth Hermitage, Northumberland*, 1779, pen, ink and watercolour (Government Art Collection)

J M W Turner (1775–1851), *Warkworth Castle, Northumberland – Thunderstorm Approaching at Sunset*, 1799, watercolour (Victoria & Albert Museum)

Whitby Abbey, North Yorkshire

ALFRED WILLIAM HUNT, an admirer of the watercolours of J M W Turner and of the Pre-Raphaelites, took the medium to its limits in seeking to capture the beauty of transient effects of light. A prize-winning student of English verse and a Fellow at Oxford University, Hunt changed career in 1861 to devote himself to art and the poetry of nature. John Ruskin praised his watercolours and he is now regarded, with Samuel Palmer, as the most successful of Turner's followers in the medium. Hunt was especially fond of Whitby. He first visited in 1874 and returned every year. His daughter recalled how 'he would find a more salubrious perch on the broad roof of Whitby station, overlooking the harbour, by special arrangement with the station master' in order to paint.

In Hunt's view from a hilltop above the houses of West Pier, he uses a high skyline and distant viewpoint to portray the abbey above a jumble of interlocking roofs. But for the time of day, it could illustrate an ideal he described in a magazine article two years later in 1880: 'Let us imagine ourselves looking at a cliff or hillside, thickly set with buildings and houses, red-roofed and many gabled, with perhaps some tower or thin-worn ruined abbey whose grey walls have been turned gold by the blaze of the sunset behind us.' The viewpoint, facing east, shows the abbey and St Mary's Church linked to the town by the arcing staircase of 199 steps; compositionally the arc continues into the Hill Pier in the centre and so to the beach where washing is drying in the sun and wind. As a mathematician and lover of music, Hunt appreciated compositional subtleties and here heeds Ruskin's advice 'to keep organisation in the midst of mystery'.

Benjamin Turner was one of Britain's first amateur photographers. Eight years after W H Fox Talbot patented his photography technique in 1841, Turner adopted his process of printing on albumen paper (paper floated on an emulsion of egg white containing light-sensitive silver salts). He produced this view of Whitby for a unique album of 60 photographs, now in the Victoria & Albert Museum, but unlike Hunt he adopted a more traditional, antiquarian viewpoint.

The ruins of Whitby Abbey stand on the headland on the south side of the old whaling port. Here in 664 the Synod of Whitby sought to reconcile the Celtic and Roman branches of the Christian church. The Benedictine abbey has been a ruin since it was dissolved in 1538, for it was stripped to provide building materials for the Cholmley family home nearby. To Hunt, as a scholar of English poetry, it would have carried further associations as the home of Caedmon (fl 670–80) the monk who wrote hymns here after being invited to join the abbey by Abbess Hild. The Venerable Bede noted that Caedmon was the first to write hymns in Old English.

Whitby has also been an inspiration to writers. C L Dodgson (Lewis Carroll) is thought to have written the story of the Walrus and the Carpenter in *Through the Looking Glass* (1872) with Whitby's sandy beach in mind, while Bram Stoker's *Dracula* (1897) includes the midnight landing of the Count from Transylvania on the shore at Whitby, from a deserted ship that ran ashore in a storm with only the corpse of its captain left on board, lashed to the wheel.

Benjamin Turner (1815–94), *Whitby Abbey from the North East*, 1852–4, albumen print from calotype negative (Victoria & Albert Museum)

Alfred William Hunt (1830–96), *Across Whitby Harbour to the Abbey*, 1878, pencil and watercolour with scratching out (Private Collection)

Witley Court, Worcestershire

WHEN QUEEN ADELAIDE, WIDOW OF KING WILLIAM IV, decided to take Witley Court as her autumn residence for three years, *The Illustrated London News* commissioned this view by J Wood to illustrate an article announcing her arrival. The artist is otherwise unknown. The anonymous article on the front page (Saturday 5 August 1843) assured its readers that the house 'is, without exception, one of the finest properties in the kingdom'. Queen Victoria's aunt was coming for her health, 'a sojourn in one of the midland counties having been recommended by her majesty's medical advisers, in lieu of the contemplated visit to Germany'.

An Italianate palace in the West Midlands, Witley Court was among the most ostentatious of Victorian country houses. Wood's watercolour shows the house as it appeared after its transformation from an enlarged Jacobean mansion around 1805–15 with the addition of Ionic porticos by John Nash. Here in the 1850s Willliam Humble Ward, 1st Earl of Dudley, spent a fortune earned in the 'Black Country' from the family's industrial empire of over 200 mines, iron-smelting works, chemical factories and a railway construction business. Their lavish country house parties flourished into the Edwardian age, despite mounting debts. Every room of the house would be filled by guests and their servants for up to a week. Edward, Prince of Wales (later King Edward VII), came regularly with his entourage for royal shooting parties. The upkeep of deer, pheasants and partridges alone required 25 full-time gamekeepers. In all, life at Witley Court required over 100 servants.

The reckless extravagance of William, 2nd Earl of Dudley (who moved in in 1888), was typical of the 'champagne Charlie' response by some irresponsible owners to the apparent end of the great tradition of the English country house. Between 1889 and 1913 Dudley mortgaged the estate and sold paintings to pay for his house parties. In 1920 he suddenly sold up when his wife Rachel drowned. Years of unpaid bills were found stuffed into urns at the foot at the main stairs, where Dudley must have left them on his way to breakfast. Nonetheless Witley Court lived on. The new owner, a Kidderminster carpet manufacturer,

Herbert 'Piggy' Smith, bought the house fully furnished and retired two years later, a self-made millionaire at 49.

In 1937 a fire destroyed part of the house and, as his insurance proved inadequate to fund the repairs, Piggy invited in the auctioneers. This classic tale of the decline of the English country house continued with the failure to find a buyer for the house and estate as a whole. Over eight days in 1938 Witley welcomed visitors of another kind, bidders at a vast auction of the house's contents and its garden ornaments. The emptied house itself finally sold in 1939 for £4,000 before the Second World War provided a stay of execution.

In 1954 Witley Court was bought by a salvage dealer who stripped the plate glass from the conservatory, the marble chimneypieces from the rooms, the lead slates and timbers from the roof, reducing the house to its bare bones. The final stages of decline, ruination and then demolition could have ensued. A motor-racing circuit, housing estate or caravan park were the best options proposed until, in 1972, a Compulsory Purchase Order by the government saved the shell of Witley Court with its gardens for the nation.

Today Witley Court is not a ruin but a dismantled house and in its skeletal state it provides a rare opportunity to study how a great building was built and has evolved, at the expense of generations of owners' fortunes. The core, from around 1600, was extended in the early 18th century in the Palladian style, when the parish church (which stands complete alongside the house) was also built. Nash added the porticos and between 1854 and 1860 Samuel Whitfield Daukes remodelled the house for William Humble Ward. The gardens were laid out by William Andrews Nesfield. His painting of the spectacular Perseus and Andromeda fountain, surrounded by flower beds, may be a proposal to win the commission from his client. As the restoration of the gardens continues, the carcass of Witley Court provides visitors with an exceptional opportunity to explore the anatomy of a great country house. The more imaginative may picture it in its heyday, while the more melancholy may muse on the folly of human endeavour, the classic response to ancient ruins.

J Wood (fl 1843), *Witley Court*, 1843, watercolour (Royal Institute of British Architects)

William Andrews Nesfield (1794–1881), *The Perseus and Andromeda Fountain, Witley Court*, 1855, watercolour (G Stansfield Collection/Nesfield Archive)

Wrest Park, Bedfordshire

THIS BIRD'S-EYE VIEW shows the former house at Wrest Park and its gardens. It is typical of the country house prospects produced by the Dutch immigrant artists Johannes Kip and Leonard Knyff for their series of 80 engravings of 66 'Palaces and noble Men's houses in England', published as *Britannia Illustrata or Views of Several of the Queen's Palaces also of the Principal Seats of the Nobility and Gentry of Great Britain* (1707). There must have been great interest in such engravings for a French edition was published in 1708. A second volume, devoted to ecclesiastical buildings and towns, appeared in 1713. As well as this engraving the volume includes a more extensive bird's-eye view of 'Wrest House and Park' and similar views of houses such as Chiswick House and Bolsover in their settings. Knyff's drawings, engraved by Kip, also led to commissions from some of the houses' owners for the same views as oil paintings.

Today the chief glory of Wrest Park remains the Great Garden created by Anthony Grey, 11th Earl of Kent and, after his death in 1702, by his son Henry, whom Queen Anne made Duke of Kent. The Duke commissioned designs from Giacomo Leoni, Nicholas Hawksmoor, James Gibbs and William Kent, but used none of them. Instead, he seems to have designed the gardens himself, with the help of his wife, his gardener and the family tutor. John Rocque's plan of 1735 was presumably made for the benefit of visitors, like his plan of the gardens at Chiswick (*see* p 40). It records the landscape centred on the axial Long Water (*c* 1685), which terminated in The Pavilion designed by Thomas Archer (1709–11), as it still does today. On the Duke's death in 1740 Wrest passed to his granddaughter Jemima (aged 17), who started the tradition of conserving the Duke's garden. Horace Walpole came to see it but found Wrest 'very ugly in the old-fashioned manner with high hedges and canals'. Lancelot 'Capability' Brown was called in to propose modifications but made only minor alterations between 1758 and 1760, softening the banks of the canals in the perimeter woodland to look more natural, doing nothing, as he said, that 'might unravel the Mystery of the Gardens'.

Like Witley Court, Wrest Park could serve as a case-study in the history of the decline of the English country house. Thomas, Earl de Grey, demolished the old home after he inherited it in 1833. Being a keen amateur architect (he was to become the first President of the Institute of British Architects) he designed the new house himself in the style of Louis XV with a formal 'French Garden' and orangery alongside.

Thomas de Grey's daughter inherited in 1859 and, in the absence of direct heirs, Wrest snaked down the inheritance ladders via a nephew and a distant cousin. From 1906 to 1911 the house was let to the American Ambassador and in the First World War it was used as a home for disabled officers (like the convalescent home established at Osborne in 1904), gaining it the affectionate title 'Wrest in Beds'. With the death of its owner, Lord Lucas, in the Royal Flying Corps in 1917, his sister sold Wrest. Trees were felled and park monuments sold. The Essex Timber Company purchased the estate in 1930 and sold it to the Sun Insurance Office in 1938. In 1946 the Ministry of Public Buildings and Works bought Wrest Park for the nation and leased the house to the National Institute of Agricultural Engineering. The successor to the NIAE was the Silsoe Research Institute, which seems fitting as de Grey devoted half his reception rooms to his library.

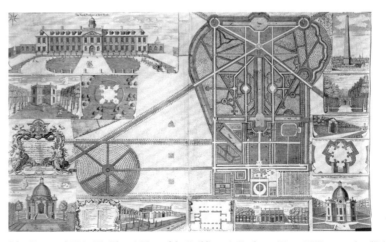

John Rocque (1704–62), *Plan & View of the Buildings & Garden at Wrest*, 1735, engraving (Private Collection)

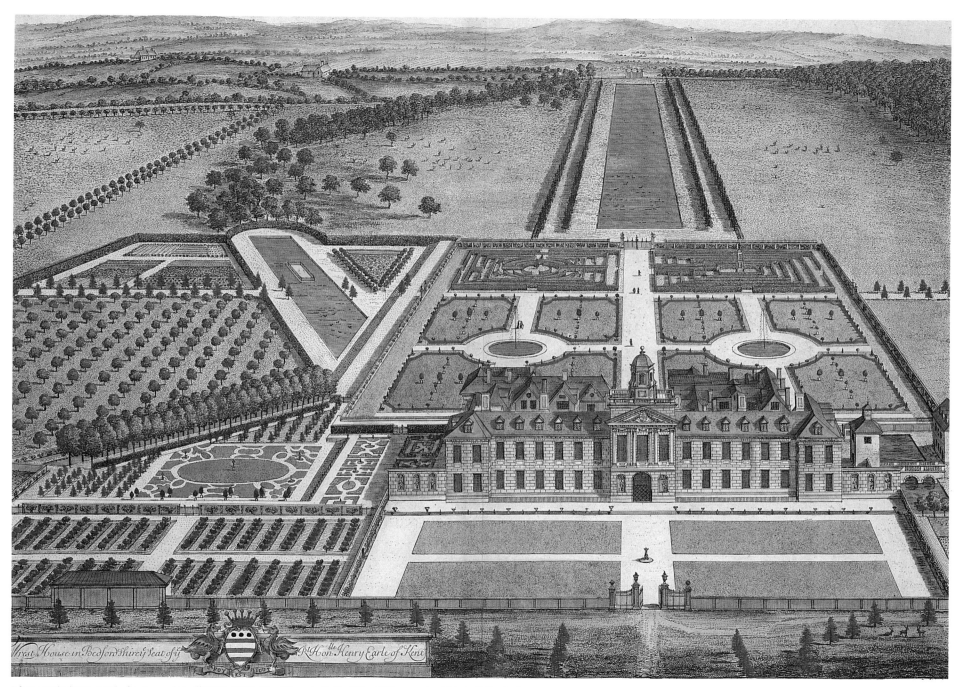

Johannes Kip (1653–1722) after Leonard Knyff (1650–1721), *Wrest House in Bedfordshire*, 1708, engraving (Private Collection)

Further reading

Andrews, M 1989 *The Search for the Picturesque. Landscape Aesthetics and Tourism in Britain, 1760–1800*. Aldershot: Scolar

Bryant, J 1986 *Finest Prospects. Three Historic Houses. A Study in London Topography*. Exhibition catalogue. London: The Iveagh Bequest, Kenwood

Bryant, J 1996 *Turner: Painting the Nation. English Heritage Properties as seen by J M W Turner*. London: English Heritage

Bryant, J 1996 'Villa views and the uninvited audience' in Arnold, D (ed) *The Georgian Villa*. Stroud: Sutton, 11–24

Bryant, J 1997 *Collections Review: An Introduction to English Heritage Museums and Collections*. London: English Heritage

Bryant, J 1997 'Madox Brown's *English Autumn Afternoon* revisited: Pre-Raphaelitism and the environment', *Apollo* CXLVI, 41–3

Charlesworth, M 1994 'The ruined abbey: Picturesque and Gothic values' in Copley, S and Garside, P (eds) *The Politics of the Picturesque*. Cambridge: Cambridge University Press, 62–80

Collins, J 1983 *Landscape in Britain 1850–1950*. Hayward Gallery exhibition catalogue. London: Arts Council of Great Britain

Conner, P 1984 *Michael Angelo Rooker: 1746–1801*. London: Batsford

Grigson, G 1975 *Britain Observed: The Landscape Through Artists' Eyes*. London: Phaidon Press

Harris, J 1979 *The Artist and the Country House*. London: Philip Wilson

Herrmann, L 1986 *Paul and Thomas Sandby*. London: Batsford

Howard, P 1985 'Painters preferred places', *Journal of Historical Geography* 11, II, 138–54

Jenkins, D F 1983 *John Piper*. Exhibition catalogue. London: Tate Gallery

Kriz, K D 1997 *The Idea of the English Landscape Painter: Genius as Alibi in the Early Nineteenth Century*. New Haven and London: Yale University Press

Macaulay, R 1953 *The Pleasure of Ruins*. London: Weidenfeld and Nicholson

Morris, D 1989 *Thomas Hearne and his Landscape*. London: Reaktion

Norden, G 2001 *Landscapes Under the Luggage Rack: Great Paintings of Britain*, 2nd ed. Northampton: Great Norden Railway Publications

Parris, L 1973 *Landscape in Britain* c 1750–1850. Exhibition catalogue. London: Tate Gallery

Peters Corbett, D, Holt, Y and Russell, F (eds) 1997 *The Geographies of Englishness. Landscape and the National Past 1880–1940*. New Haven and London: Yale University Press

Rosenthal, M, Payne, C and Wilcox, S (eds) 1997 *Prospects for the Nation: Recent Essays in British Landscape, 1750–1880*. New Haven and London: Yale University Press

Smiles, S 1994 *The Image of Antiquity. Ancient Britain and the Romantic Imagination*. New Haven and London: Yale University Press

Sweet, R 2004 *Antiquaries. The Discovery of the Past in Eighteenth-Century Britain*. London: Hambledon

Timmers, M (ed) 1998 *The Power of the Poster*. Exhibition catalogue. London: Victoria & Albert Museum Publications

Tinniswood, A 1989 *A History of Country House Visiting: Five Centuries of Tourism and Taste*. Oxford: Basil Blackwell

Woodbridge, K 1970 *Landscape and Antiquity: Aspects of English Culture at Stourhead, 1718 to 1838*. Oxford: Clarendon Press

Woodward, C 2001 *In Ruins*. London: Chatto & Windus

Illustration credits

All photographs of the sites are © English Heritage, with the exception of the following: © Andrew Tryner: 36; © David Garner: 90, 110; © Jeremy Young: 40; © John Critchley: 28, 74; Landguard Fort Trust: 78; © Paul Highnam: 128; © Skyscan Balloon Photography: 18, 80, 92, 98, 116, 130.

Unless otherwise noted, all illustrations are reproduced by permission of English Heritage. Other illustrations are reproduced by kind permission of the following:

Aberdeen Art Gallery & Museums Collections: 69

Anthony Mould Ltd: 78, 79

Art Archive: 24

Barry Martin: 19

Bedfordshire & Luton Archives & Records Service: 130

Birmingham Museum & Art Gallery: 91

Bodleian Library, Oxford: 34

Bridgeman Art Library: 48, 119 (Ashmolean Museum, University of Oxford, UK); 89 (British Museum, London, UK); 82 (Fitzwilliam Museum, University of Cambridge, UK); 12 (Guildhall Library, Corporation of London, UK); 16 (© David Inshaw); 68t (Ironbridge Gorge Museum, Telford, Shropshire, UK); 30 (© Leeds Museums and Galleries (City Art Gallery), UK); 103 (Museum of London, UK); 33, 95 (Norfolk Museums Service (Norwich Castle Museum), UK); 6t, 9b, 16, 23, 32, 112, 113 (Private Collection); 49 (Private Collection, Bonhams, London, UK); 68b (Private Collection, Chris Beetles, London, UK); 131 (Private Collection, The Stapleton Collection); 117 (St Faith's Church, Gaywood, Norfolk, UK); 35, 93, 100, 115 (Victoria & Albert Museum, London, UK); fc, 5, 20, 59, 61, 71, 107, 111, 116 (© Yale Center for British Art, Paul Mellon Collection, USA); 101, 105 (© Yale Center for British Art, Paul Mellon Fund, USA); 53, 77 (York Museums Trust (York Art Gallery), UK)

British Library: 104 (Cotton MS Faustina B VII, fol 85v), 121

Cheltenham Art Gallery & Museum: 118

Christie's Images Ltd 2005: 83, 87, 127

English Heritage/The Earl of Mansfield, Scone Palace: 73

English Heritage/Private Collection: 15, 18, 65, 66, 67, 72r, 74

G Stansfield Collection/Nesfield Archive: 129b

Greenwich Local History Library: 102

Manchester Art Gallery: 90

Mary Evans Picture Library: 108 (British Library), 109 (British Library)

National Gallery of Ireland: 51

© National Maritime Museum, London: 99

NRM/Pictorial Collection/Science & Society Picture Library: 7l, 9t, 36r, 38r, 62, 106

National Trust Photographic Library: 63, 64 (John Hammond)

Private Collection: 7r, 38l

© Queen's Printer and Controller of HMSO, 2005 UK Government Art Collection: 45, 124

RIBA Library Drawings Collection: 129t

Royal Collection © 2005 Her Majesty Queen Elizabeth II: 27, 44, 97

© Royal Institution of Cornwall: 55

Shell Art Collection, National Motor Museum: 94b, 114

Sotheby's: 57, 80, 120

© Tate London 2005: 17, 21, 54, 86, 94t, 98

Tullie House Museum & Art Gallery, Carlisle: 36l, 37

Victoria & Albert Museum: 6b, 13l, 125, 126

Weidenfeld Ltd: 2

Whitworth Art Gallery, University of Manchester: 31, 39

The Wordsworth Trust: 56

Worth B Stottlemeyer Collection, Juniata College Museum of Art, Huntingdon, Pennsylvania, USA: 70

York Museums Trust: 42, 43 (Reproduced by courtesy of the Lowry Estate)

Index of illustrations: artists

Index of illustrations: sites